Shell Shocked Britain

Shell Shocked Britain

The First World War's Legacy for Britain's Mental Health

Suzie Grogan

PEN & SWORD
HISTORY

First published in Great Britain in 2014 by
Pen & Sword History
an imprint of
Pen & Sword Books Ltd
47 Church Street
Barnsley
South Yorkshire
S70 2AS

ISBN 978 1 78159 265 6

A CIP catalogue record for this book is available from the British
Library

Typeset in Ehrhardt by
Mac Style Ltd, Bridlington, East Yorkshire
Printed and bound in the UK by CPI Group (UK) Ltd, Croydon,
CRO 4YY

Pen & Sword Books Ltd incorporates the imprints of Pen & Sword
Archaeology, Atlas, Aviation, Battleground, Discovery, Family
History, History, Maritime, Military, Naval, Politics, Railways,
Select, Transport, True Crime, and Fiction, Frontline Books, Leo
Cooper, Praetorian Press, Seaforth Publishing and Wharncliffe.

For a complete list of Pen & Sword titles please contact
PEN & SWORD BOOKS LIMITED
47 Church Street, Barnsley, South Yorkshire, S70 2AS, England
E-mail: enquiries@pen-and-sword.co.uk
Website: www.pen-and-sword.co.uk

Contents

Acknowledgements

Many people have offered support in the writing of this book. In particular I would like to thank Dr Peter Heinl for his inspirational discussion on the subject of trans-generational trauma and Richard Van Emden for his time and for his wonderful work in the field of oral history. Thanks also to Patrick Baty for a twenty-first century perspective on the experience of the soldier, to Ian Stevenson for his support on the subject of inter-war psychotherapy and to all those who have allowed me to share their family stories in this book. I am also indebted to the staff at the Wellcome, British and London Libraries, The Liddle Collection at the University of Leeds and The National Archives.

A special thank you to Amy Gregor at The British Newspaper Archive for her permission to use images from the archive and to Nick Tomlinson at Picture the Past, The North East Midlands Photographic Record, a not-for-profit project that aims to make historic images from the library and museum collections across Derbyshire and Nottinghamshire available via *www.picturethepast.org.uk*. His generous agreement to the use of images and postcards from the site has proved invaluable. Much of this book was written away from home to avoid my tendency to procrastinate and so my love and thanks go to Kate Flint and Adam Grogan, and to the whole of the Lake District for enabling me to concentrate on getting the words out of my head on to paper.

A special mention for my editor, Jen Newby formerly of Pen & Sword History, who has been a source of endless support and to my husband and family who have lived with this book for the past 18 months.

For Peter, James and Evie, my little family full of love; and for my mother, Stella Furneaux, for her love, support and contribution to everything good in me.

Chapter One

Introduction

This book is to be neither an accusation nor a confession, and least of all an adventure, for death is not an adventure to those who stand face to face with it. It will try simply to tell of a generation of men who, even though they may have escaped shells, were destroyed by the war.

(Erich Maria Remarque, *All Quiet on the Western Front 1929*)

What exactly was 'shell shock'? Was it an individual diagnosis, simply a very personal tragedy affecting an individual soldier and his family? During and after the First World War, was the condition simply a matter for the military; for medical and pension boards, official inquiries or an issue for regiments and officers struggling to increase the number, effectiveness and morale of troops facing desperate months in the trenches? Should we extend the term to civilians; whole communities, villages, towns and cities left to live with the loss of thousands of young, fit men? Can we make a case for a 'shell shocked nation'?

It is not an easy assertion to make. Criticism has been levelled at academics claiming that war trauma spread beyond those on the front line, experiencing combat at first-hand, to civilians at home, fearing invasion or air raids, or the loss of loved ones. In her 2009 book, *Aftershocks*, Susan Kingsley Kent argues that in 1920s Britain these various degrees of trauma developed into a collective fear of imagined enemies. This fear resulted in violence against, for example, Jewish communities, Irish nationalists and Bolsheviks in the General Strike of 1926. Newspaper reports of the time support her view that the war had long-lasting psychological effects on both soldiers and civilians.

This book does not seek to prove a clear, collective response. There is no evidence to show that any hysterical reaction affected the population in large enough numbers to undermine Britain's national identity. Instead, *Shell Shocked Britain* offers an insight into the trauma and chronic anxiety experienced during the First World War by sufficient numbers of the population, both combatants and civilians, to leave a permanent legacy. It shows how this anxiety transformed attitudes to and treatment of mental health throughout the inter-war period, the different ways in which men, women and children experienced this trauma and how it changed roles and relationships well into the twentieth century.

Social history and personal memoirs can offer opportunities to consider how the common experience of trauma and anxiety influenced official, medical and public responses to mental illness. Families lived through uncertain times during the twentieth century, as the convictions of the Victorian and Edwardian eras were grasped and then discarded. The arguments surrounding the 'right' way to approach a mental health issue – even the recognition of certain behaviours – rage on into the twenty-first century. However, as this book shows, the roots of modern mental health treatments are embedded in the inter-war response to the emotional upheaval that began in 1914. The term 'shell shock' is, to a twenty-first century audience, synonymous with the First World War, trench warfare, mud and blood and the deaths of millions of young men.

By the time of the Armistice, the British Army had identified and treated approximately 80,000 young men for shell shock, however, this is a gross underestimate of the total actually affected. For example, if a man were physically and mentally wounded, only the physical wound was recorded. Despite evidence given at later medical boards and inquiries, it was clear to many that 'war neurosis' (as the condition was also called) affected combatants across all classes and ethnic backgrounds. Previously fit men experienced debilitating symptoms. They may have had continuous diarrhoea, nervous tics, paralysis and blindness, while they also became disorientated, hysterical or withdrawn. Nightmares tormented the little sleep they could get; for some eating and drinking was impossible. Anxiety was acute and relentless, and nervous collapse inevitable for many in the face of constant bombardment by the enemy; the knowledge that one must kill or be killed and the obliteration of close comrades.

The term 'shell shock' was coined by the medical profession in the conflict of 1914–18. The phrase helped those involved in the consequences of the war to express the sheer scale of the battles, the horror of industrialised warfare, the loss and the terror. It distinguished the First World War from previous wars in which the soldier was a professional and the enemy in plain sight, to be engaged in anticipated combat. Yet, as a concept, 'shell shock' also became a barrier. The soldier with direct experience of front line combat was in some sense alienated from his physicians, from the bureaucratic military boards which decided on his fitness for active service and ultimately from those he loved and was closest to. Millions of people waved away a smiling, fit youth and welcomed home someone physically present but seemingly lost to them in every other way.

Professor Jay Winter, author of the deeply moving and magisterial *Sites of Memory, Sites of Mourning*, has argued that 'shell-shock' could be a peculiarly British construct; initially a medical way of describing a form of nervous collapse or 'neurasthenia' more readily attributed before the war to women. Professor Winter points out that there is no direct translation of the term into other European languages. Is this, he asks, because in Europe war veterans enjoyed far greater influence on political life? In Britain, veterans' organisations, such as the British Legion, were apolitical and more akin to pre-war friendly societies. As all attempts to involve veterans in a national movement withered away, no high profile nationwide organisation emerged to uphold the national 'soldierly spirit', which had supported many through the horrors of the war itself.

Shell shock, from its earliest published description in *The Lancet* in 1915, has always been a cultural rather than a medical construct. It offered safety to thousands of physically healthy young men suffering from some indefinable and incomprehensible mental problem. During the war it was still widely believed that to be 'shell shocked' a soldier must have received an injury due to proximity to an exploding shell, with the blast causing their symptoms. It took some time for medical officers to link the term to the psychological effects of war-enduring a constant barrage of shell fire, the fear of imminent death and the impact of the loss of comrades. In the meantime, the term helped soldiers plead for financial support, medical assistance and understanding from an otherwise bemused and possibly cynical society.

It must also be recognised that our understanding of shell shock is primarily based on the evidence of a middle and upper class elite, those young men of the officer class (who in relative terms suffered most acutely from mental trauma in the Great War), who expressed their fears in poetry and prose, in music and in artworks depicting the horror and destruction. They used art in its broadest sense to describe experiences they could not otherwise voice. The wider working class narrative of war has emerged during the more recent move to oral and social history across all classes. One hundred years on from the Great War, it is increasingly seen as important to raise awareness and 'democratise' mental illness. Today we recognise that it can strike anyone.

Is shell shock now a cultural construct? The traumatised soldier has become an iconic figure, from early, silent French films such as *J'Accuse* (1919) to the point of lampooning in the BBC TV comedy *Blackadder Goes Forth*? How far can the term be applied not just to the soldiers on the front line, but to the country as a whole? To the communities those soldiers belonged to and the families who had to live through four years of ever more desperate warfare? After all, the English Channel was not the insurmountable barrier many politicians assumed it would be. In 1914 there was a belief that Britannia would always 'rule the waves' and the establishment was so certain that right was on its side that young cavalry officers were sent into battle against tanks and machine guns. By the end of the war, the skies above Britain were becoming as important a battleground as the fields of Flanders or the waters around their 'Sceptred Isle'.

Before we make assumptions about the traumatising effect of war on the social fabric of the nation, or see shell shock reverberating through the inter-war years, it is important to acknowledge that not everybody exhibited the classic signs of emotional distress linked to war trauma. Many soldiers came back from the Front exhausted, drained, but essentially in one piece physically and mentally. Some were even excited and exhilarated by their experience; panic and anxiety attacks severe enough to disrupt daily existence were not the norm. Certainly many ex-soldiers and civilians went on to live happy and fulfilling lives, re-marrying and rebuilding their trust in the State and the nation sufficiently to encourage husbands, sons, and eventually mothers, wives and daughters, to take a role in the next great conflict just 20 years later.

Towards the end of the war there was much discussion in the press about the incidence of 'nerves', 'neurosis' and 'mental defectives' within the general population. Doctors were concerned about a possible increase in the numbers committed to asylums as a direct consequence of stresses on the Home Front. Parallels were not drawn with any discussion of shell shock or war neurosis amongst the troops. In June 1918, the Central Board of Control for Scotland reported that the war 'had the effect of decreasing the number of lunatics among the civil population' – a fact that came as a surprise to many. The authors reported that doctors had anticipated a surge in numbers, 'due to the immense though unconscious mental strain' the population was under. Pressure on parents and wives when their sons and husbands were away fighting, bereavement and the general privations of wartime were among the many reasons why the Board had expected to see a rise in the numbers of those 'breaking down'.

The report suggested a number of possible reasons for this unexpected result. Firstly, they noted that during the war there had been a reduction in unemployment and a general rise in income levels, but this had largely benefited the working classes and the numbers of middle and upper class 'lunatics' had dropped too. So they came to the following conclusion: 'it will be found in that sub-conscious excitement by which nature is accustomed to key up the physical and intellectual powers to meet an extraordinary strain … the war by providing an inducement to sustained effort in its achievement of a clearly defined objective has given us a partial solution to the lunacy problem.'

No one would suggest war is the solution to the problems of society, but the 1914–1918 conflict seemed to have alleviated some of the strains caused by unemployment, financial worries and other practical matters which are recognised causes of serious mental stress. In addition, at times of trauma and anxiety the 'flight or fight' response is activated. Although these effects are common to us all, some people are better able to manage the symptoms produced – increased heart-rate, respiration and blood pressure. Those prone to panic attacks find this natural survival instinct can also cause the symptoms of hyperventilation, palpitations and ringing in the ears. The 1918 report describes how many Britons were sustained throughout the war by a feeling of common purpose and the sub-conscious excitement, which enabled them to meet an 'extraordinary strain'. The term 'flight or fight' was not coined until 1932, but this concept appears to be what the Board was describing. What then happened to the post-war British population, when that 'inducement to sustained effort' was no longer there?

This book aims to re-examine some of the longer-term responses to the war and its consequences for British people. Historians such as Martin Pugh in *We Danced All Night* (2008) have proposed that Britain's post-war response, contrary to popular myth, was remarkably positive. During the Roaring Twenties people partied, drank, spent money on new goods in a wider variety of shops; they worked, lived, loved, married and had children with new freedoms and greater opportunities.

However, modern advances in psychiatric research and in psychotherapy practice highlight the many different reactions to trauma and show these post-war behaviours in a different light. Behavioural patterns change; promiscuity increases and spending levels go up, for example, as caution is lost and consequences denied. By acting in this way, an individual could be seeking to dissociate themselves from the horror they have experienced and the anxiety and depression they battle. The stoicism and silence that we might attribute to 'stiff upper lip' can be explained by a lack of vocabulary to describe their experiences. The world had indeed changed yet it would take time for the language to change with it.

The picture of life in Britain after the First World War is a complex one. To fully grasp it we have to look more widely at our sources and appreciate recent oral history and examination of contemporaneous diaries and letters. Above all, we must be willing to set aside our preconceived ideas about the mental state of the nation after 1918.

Historically it is generally agreed that the Great War intervened between a society clinging to an increasingly irrelevant Victorian moral code and one less at ease with the inequalities that it perpetrated. The move towards a world offering greater equality in the relationship between state and individual, employer and employee, and at the micro level, between individual men and women, made slow progress until after the Second World War. Yet the State was already becoming more closely involved with the lives of ordinary people and it is interesting to consider how far the Great War hastened that change. What impact did change have on the lives of families to whom soldiers returned after discharge or demobilisation? Was Britain after 1918 a country struggling to deal with death and the end of a social order, or was it one, as historian Martin Pugh suggests, that 'danced all night'?

At the heart of this issue also lies the question of whether soldiers were the only victims of shell-shock or if Britain itself was left reeling, uncertain and on the brink of social unrest. Pre-war concerns relating to Irish nationalism, violent protests from militant suffragettes and from a burgeoning labour movement, the possibility of strikes and violent confrontations with employers and the state – all were suspended as the war re-affirmed the importance of patriotism and nationhood. How far were these fears revived post-war, and did a national sense of anxiety reinforce a feeling of despair in the general population, including the troops demobilised between 1918 and 1920? What was the mood of the country?

Many of the wartime experiences that tipped apparently strong, brave men back into a state of child-like helplessness are primeval ones at the root of all our fears, even today. We still have nightmares about being buried alive, of being deafened by noise or half-drowned; these are methods of torture still regularly utilised in some parts of the world to obtain information or confession. Finding the right language when faced with the death of someone close is a source of deep sorrow and the sight of bodies blown apart, limbs separated, faces burned, is still part of our indirect collective experience. Terrorist attacks on civilians in Western cities and horrific injuries to serving soldiers are given attention by an occasionally prurient media, while other atrocities on a global stage go unreported.

As we look back over 100 years, our 'nameless dread' may be different and our anxieties evoked by other sources, but the sense in which the soldiers, medical establishment, families and society as a whole came to terms with the trauma of 1914–1918 still resonates. The First World War brought psychoanalysis to the mainstream and posed challenges to the medical profession which it struggled to meet. There is little doubt that everyone surviving World War One was traumatised to some extent. Some responded to the healing rituals of mourning and remembrance better than others, but there is enough evidence of certain behaviours throughout the inter-war years to suggest that thousands, perhaps hundreds of thousands were sufficiently damaged for it to adversely affect the rest of their lives. As it did so, the war also had an impact on their children; they, in turn, passed on the consequences of their experience to the next generation.

Inevitably, the Great War has become a myth for the majority, too young to have experienced conflict on a foreign field or home front. Names on war memorials are reduced to symbols and remembrance becomes an abstract idea – moving on to include, rightly, more recent conflicts. Perhaps a danger inherent in referring to this book as a 'history of a nation traumatised' is that we lose sight of the individuals who played their part in the story. I hope I have included enough of the individual experiences of soldiers and their families to ensure that is not the case, but there will never be enough space to properly reflect the ways in which so many suffered. We must always recognise their presence.

As we rightly say 'lest we forget', we have to remember why the suffering of so many of those men was, and still is, forgotten, as mental illness remains a taboo subject, particularly for those currently serving in war zones around the world. To remove the stigma, shouldn't we show the shell shocked to the nation?

This book was inspired by a particular incident in my own family history. A great-uncle on my maternal side, Alfred Hardiman, was by all accounts a gentle, mild-mannered man. Relatively short and slightly built, he lived with his mother in Hornsey, North London. Alfred, aged 27 at the start of the war, was conscripted in 1916 and discharged 'unfit for active service', just 10 months later. In December 1922, just after Christmas, he stood in the kitchen of his family home, grabbed his ex-girlfriend – a friend of his sister, who also lodged with the family – and cut her throat with a razor, almost severing her head. He then turned the razor on himself and slashed his own throat. Within seconds they both lay dead on the floor.

Alfred's sister was my grandmother Bessie Hardiman, she witnessed the whole event. She was also a key witness at the subsequent inquest, at which it was revealed that Alfred had been caught in one of the Gotha air raids on London in 1917 and subsequently spent a year in an unidentified, but almost certainly psychiatric, hospital. His mother Clara told the inquest that he had 'never been the same since', and reports show that he suffered from periods of depression. The coroner found Alfred guilty of the murder and suicide 'whilst of unsound mind' and this horrific event, although it was explored within the national press, was consequently hushed up by the family. My mother, born just seven years later, knew nothing of it until I happened upon a cutting in *The Times* by chance, in 2005. Over 80 years after the event she was able to trace the consequences of Alfred's actions across and down the generations. Bessie Hardiman married her long-term fiancé within three months of the event, and one of her brothers also married. A sister had a breakdown 10 years later and became addicted to gambling, ruining her family. Two of Alfred's sisters ended their lives in mental hospitals in the 1960s and 1970s, while Alfred's nephew had a breakdown and died aged just 49. My mother herself suffers from acute anxiety and now sees the pattern repeated in my own experience of depression and anxiety.

Of course, it would be impossible to prove that any of this was a direct consequence of Alfred Hardiman's involvement in the First World War, but the suppression of emotion was a common response to trauma after the war ended. Acts of remembrance were not universally acknowledged to be a good idea, in case the British stiff upper lip should be encouraged to waver once more. Work undertaken by psychologist Dr Peter Heinl across communities in Europe suggests that even now direct experience of the Second World War as a child can impact on the adult psyche, even if the early horrors are not immediately recalled. His use of family trees to support clients working with family trauma often identifies the impact of the Great War across three generations.

Neither is there a clear boundary between the Front line and Home Front experience. Troops were faced with situations of indescribable horror, and were subject to long periods of intense anxiety and hours of ear-splitting bombardment by enemy shells, yet the loneliness, the 'not knowing', the guilt of the survivor, all had a psychological impact, too. On the Home Front, British women, and those men unable to be part of the direct war effort, were largely fighting different battles, but they were not sheltered from psychological trauma. It is impossible to deny the impact of the first industrialised warfare; death was brought to British doorsteps by the dreaded telegram, by the newspapers, and in some cases by the bombs dropped from airships and planes, or fired from German ships. To expect those who witnessed events of indescribable horror to continue undamaged is to deny our humanity and has put intense pressure on thousands to repress memories that required expression in order to properly heal.

Very little work was undertaken after the war to investigate its impact on those who had managed on the Home Front. British priorities were elsewhere and acts of remembrance were relied upon to heal wounds. However, experiences detailed in oral history and studies of the Great War suggest that, even decades after the war, veterans were reliving the battles they fought night after night in their dreams. As they became older, they found it easier to talk, perhaps confiding in grandchildren in a way they could not speak to their children and the stories they told were a kind of therapy; an opportunity to relive and make sense of their experiences. Increased interest in the Great War later in the twentieth century and organised tours of the battlefields also offered release.

This book is not only a sincere appreciation and testament to the bravery and suffering of the shell shocked soldiers who had to find ways to return to some sort of normality after the war, and were frequently unable to do so. It is a recognition that the indomitable British spirit so frequently depicted in the media and propaganda of the first half of the twentieth century is not the whole story.

The Great War transformed all our lives, and had a significant impact on the ways in which we approach mental health issues in modern Britain.

Suzie Grogan, October 2014

Chapter Two

A Short History of Shell Shock

After countless representations of shell shock in film, fiction and drama, if we have a picture of a shell shocked soldier it is usually of a man shaking, twisted and hunched, staring unseeing into the distance. If we hear him at all, then he is stuttering, or shrieking at intervals; crying out from nightmares relived nightly. However, in reality shell shocked men presented with so many different mental wounds that the term quickly became problematic for the medical establishment. By the end of the war some 80,000 men had been diagnosed with shell shock. Many more would have suffered mental trauma without reaching a crisis point or exhibiting obvious symptoms.

Still a challenge to military medicine today, with 'neurasthenia', 'war trauma' and conditions now known as 'post-traumatic stress' and 'combat stress', shell shock has become representative of the horrors of war and the acute and long-term pressures combatants have experienced. No longer simply a medical term reflecting the symptoms of individuals, it is also used to describe the suffering of all men at war and the disillusionment of those who had first seen the conflict as a noble campaign. It gradually became a way to re-define the post-war relationship between men and women and has been used in recent years to re-frame the ways in which gender historians approach the history of war. Were the thousands of men diagnosed with shell shock actually experiencing hysteria, that pre-war condition supposedly the sole domain of women? Was the 'heroic ideal' always a myth?

Before discussing how the nation as a whole responded to the First World War it is important to examine how our understanding of the trauma of war has changed in the last 100 years. Over the past century, the way society deals with the distress experienced by members of the Armed Forces has changed significantly, but many still feel the lack of a proper understanding of how trauma manifests itself. Substance abuse, domestic violence, unemployment – all of these problems affect ex-service personnel, but are not always connected to underlying mental health issues. When linked to the experience of war, military psychologists have to take these matters more seriously. The number of ex-soldiers now part of the prison population has been estimated, by research undertaken at criminal justice group No Offence, at 10 per cent, rather than the 3.4 per cent in official, government figures. An all-party parliamentary committee has been established to address the issue of veterans in the justice system.

The Oxford English Dictionary defines shell shock as: 'psychological disturbance caused by prolonged exposure to active warfare, especially being under bombardment'. To be 'shell shocked' is also described as being 'shocked or confused because of a sudden alarming experience'. This, the dictionary states, includes the following example: 'he told shell shocked investors that the company needed still more money to survive the year'. This definition highlights how cultural associations with the term have changed over the century. The term was first used in the First World War, but even Charles Myers, the doctor who coined it, quickly realised that it was not an accurate term to describe the myriad ways in which a man could be affected. 'Shell shock' as a concept has since entered the language to describe even the least desperate of emotions. Sports people describe themselves as 'shell shocked' by an unexpected win; a newspaper might term someone 'shell shocked' after hearing that their mild-mannered neighbour was actually a serial killer. In order to understand the seriousness of war trauma, it is important to reclaim its meaning with reference to the collective experience in the First World War.

In 1915, on volunteering for active service, Charles Myers, a Professor of Anthropology, was given a commission and sent to France to support the men suffering from this mystery condition. He is believed to have used the term 'shell shock' officially for the first time in an article published in *The Lancet* in 1915. Nevertheless, as more victims passed through the field hospitals, Myers began to have doubts about the value of the phrase. Many had been nowhere near a shell, yet were experiencing the same symptoms as those physically affected by an explosion; finding themselves deaf, blind or unable to stop shaking. In the early days of the war some physicians considered the symptoms to be a 'percussive' response, caused by the reverberations of the shellfire, but as the war progressed it became clear that shell shock had originated hundreds of years before the Great War.

The Experience of Shell Shock Before the Great War

The term shell shock was first coined in World War One, but the condition was certainly not new. Before the twentieth century, psychology did not recognise the effects of constant heavy and industrialised bombardment as the basis of a diagnosis, because these conditions simply had not been an acknowledged part of the theatre of war. In Britain, the common term 'hysteria' as a diagnosis of mental illness was confined to women, and if applied to men was seen as a slur on their masculinity. On the continent, most notably in France, it had been long recognised that men could be susceptible to mental fragility and that the attendant symptoms, although prompted by different kinds of trauma, were not gender specific. Previous battle situations had produced their own horrors to turn men's minds.

Wherever conflict occurred there would be reports of men who suffered from terror, both on the field of battle and long afterwards. Greek historians recognised symptoms of what we now understand as combat stress in the great battles of antiquity: soldiers could become blind, deaf or paralysed when witnessing the death of a comrade at close proximity. Herodotus writes of one soldier, Aristodemus, nicknamed 'The Trembler', who eventually hanged himself, too ashamed to face his comrades. During the American Civil War, the much-criticised Major Marcus Reno, whose battalion served to support Major General Custer at the battle of Little Big Horn, was said to have started yelling incomprehensible orders, rolling his eyes and running away when his Indian scout, Bloody Knife, was shot in the face, his blood and brains splattering Reno's skin.

Reports following the Thirty Years' War, which raged across Europe between 1618 and 1648, mentioned a condition affecting Spanish soldiers called 'Estar Roto', meaning 'to be crushed', 'broken' or 'in despair'. In the same war, German soldiers suffered similarly, as Catholic fought Protestant across the continent, and their symptoms were referred to as 'heimweh' – homesickness. Trauma was an unsurprising consequence of the last major religious war on the continent, which bankrupted nations and decimated populations across Europe.

In the Napoleonic Wars, troops experienced 'nostalgia', lingering psychological damage as a consequence of war, and in the American Civil War, between 1861 and 1875, 'Da Costa's Syndrome' was first recognised. Named after Jacob Mendes Da Costa, who first described the condition, it seemed to mimic a heart complaint, but without the necessary physiological problems. Now it is recognised as an anxiety disorder and has also been referred to as 'irritable heart', 'effort syndrome' and 'Soldier's Heart'.

Da Costa's syndrome was diagnosed when soldiers presented with chest pains, palpitations, breathlessness, and fatigue. The Civil War, in which conditions could be intolerable and resembled the trench warfare of the Great War, caused soldiers to break down with 'mind wounds'. Some sympathetic physicians recognised that even the bravest man could collapse under the strain. Symptoms were thought to have been caused by soldiers having to over-exert themselves and exacerbated by too little rest and poor food. Other physicians offered less compassion and soldiers were dealt with as lunatics or as malingerers. There were simply no words available to describe the pain the men were experiencing and army discipline required a firm hand. One surgeon on the Union side, William Hammond, worked hard to understand why men presented with symptoms of paralysis, nightmares and palpitations. He came to the conclusion that many soldiers were too young, too immature for battle and should never have been passed fit to serve.

Stress in combat has also been the subject of literature. Through the voice of Kate, Hotspur's wife in *Henry IV, Pt1*, Shakespeare gives us a description of the symptoms of combat stress more than three centuries before it was first properly identified:

> *Why dost thou bend thine eyes upon the earth,*
> *And start so often when thou sit'st alone?*
> *Why hast thou lost the fresh blood in thy cheeks;*
> *And given my treasures and my rights of thee*
> *To thick-eyed musing and curst melancholy?*
> *In thy faint slumbers I by thee have watch'd,*
> *And heard thee murmur tales of iron wars;*
> *Speak terms of manage [horsemanship] to thy bounding steed;*
> *Cry 'Courage! to the field!' And thou hast talk'd*

Of sallies and retires, of trenches, tents ...
... Of prisoners' ransom and of soldiers slain,
And all the currents of a heady fight.
Thy spirit within thee hath been so at war,
And thus hath so bestirr'd thee in thy sleep,
That beads of sweat have stood upon thy brow
Like bubbles in a late-disturbed stream;
And in thy face strange motions have appear'd,
Such as we see when men restrain their breath ...

In the late nineteenth and early twentieth century, up to the beginning of World War One, the asylum population in Britain was growing at an alarming rate. The increase had stretched the public asylums, built with some care in the nineteenth century, and many became overcrowded, with rudimentary treatment and regimes 'more suited to prisons than hospitals. The stereotypical picture of an asylum patient, bolstered by mid–nineteenth century literature such as *The Woman in White* by Wilkie Collins and Mr Rochester's mad wife in *Jane Eyre*, is female, perhaps incarcerated for conditions easily treated today, or merely because they were an inconvenience to their families. Men outnumbered women in private establishments, but in 1870 figures showed that in public asylums there were approximately 1,200 female to 1,000 male patients. Psychiatrists or doctors in charge of their care were considered by many in the more widely respected field of neurology as simple gaolers. They had little time to spend with each patient and few opportunities to undertake any research that could have furthered a medical breakthrough. Patients, once committed, were burdened with the stigma and shame for the rest of their lives; hardly a situation likely to prompt a complete recovery. Yearly statistics suggest that people were as likely to die in many asylums as they were to be released.

Before 1914, the treatment of those with mental illness – whether of a type understood (such as general paralysis of the insane, the term often used for the final stages of syphilis) or still little studied (such as postnatal depression) was often class-based. A large proportion of those in state-run asylums may as well have been consigned to leper colonies, for all the contact and concern they received from the wider community. Asylum patients were, in some cases, shunned and feared; assumed to be dangerous to others or to themselves and often disowned by even their closest family members. Those with sufficient wealth, who found themselves burdened with a spouse or a child exhibiting mystifying symptoms, could avoid the stigma by paying for specialist care in discreet private hospitals. The patients were labelled 'neurasthenic' rather than 'insane' and offered the latest 'spa cures' developed overseas.

As more detail was steadily uncovered about the workings of the brain, doctors drew fresh conclusions from physical examinations of dissected brains and horrific experiments on animals. They discovered new facets of organic diseases previously considered the result of madness, such as the last stages of syphilis. These findings led on to assumptions about hereditary insanity and the physical causes of madness which would confuse doctors faced with early shell shock in 1914. A shell shocked man was unlikely to have been the first case of madness most doctors would have seen, but the pressures of the war created a novel context within which these men were breaking down.

Before 1914 the causes of breakdown had already been the subject of much discussion in medical circles. In France, Jean-Martin Charcot, Professor of Neurology at the Salpetriere in Paris, was keen to show that hysteria and the typical hysterical reaction was not confined to the female sex. As previously mentioned, in Britain hysteria was frequently associated with menstruation and childbearing. In the early twentieth century American doctors were beginning to identify a new type of nervous disorder, which related to an inability to deal with the realities of life in a quickly advancing modern society. They saw mental breakdown as a response to, or an escape from, industrialisation and a faster pace of life.

Eventually, these less clearly defined conditions became known as neurosis and led to treatments ranging from a milk diet to hypnosis and 'suggestion', which, doctors claimed, could offer a complete cure. French psychologist Pierre Janet, a pioneer in the field of psychotherapy, was the first to use the term 'dissociation' to distinguish between the subconscious and conscious parts of the brain and to recognise that a past trauma could connect to a patient's current mental condition. He had not taken his theory forward however, when Sigmund Freud presented his findings on the brain's ability to repress painful memories. As these psychotherapeutic concepts still cause division and confusion in the twenty-first century it is unsurprising that, in 1914, there was disagreement, denial and ultimately experimentation on seriously damaged young men.

Although, before the war, military medicine was more concerned with venereal disease and the diseases of the tropics than with the state of soldiers' nerves, those doctors who had studied military history or the move to mechanised warfare had sufficient precedents to draw on when they encountered shell shock. In Britain, soldiers had already exhibited symptoms, such as those of Da Costa's Syndrome, which would be reclassified as an anxiety disorder in the mid-twentieth century. Between 1864 and 1868, British politician George Robinson, Earl de Grey, reported the high incidence of British soldiers with palpitations, breathlessness and chest pains, but attributed these symptoms to the weight of the military equipment the soldiers were forced to carry. In 1870 Arthur Bowen Myers of the Coldstream Guards also regarded the weight of a knapsack as the cause of 'neuro-circulatory asthenia' and 'cardiovascular neurosis'.

In the twenty-first century, academics in the United States examining soldiers' compensation claims for Post-Traumatic Stress Disorder, reported that: 'Being able to attribute 'soldier's heart' to a physical cause' provided an 'honourable solution' to all vested parties. It left the self-respect of the soldier intact and military authorities did not have to explain 'psychological breakdowns in previously brave soldiers'. Neither did they have to account for 'such troublesome issues as cowardice, low unit morale, poor leadership, or the meaning of the war effort itself'. This view prevailed at the start of the Great War.

It is possible that the first recorded modern diagnosis of something akin to shell shock was made in the Russo-Japanese War, which took place during 1904 and 1905. Early trench warfare, heavy bombardment and siege conditions created an environment that was a direct precursor of the circumstances experienced by First World War combatants. Medical reports suggest that more than 2,000 soldiers were treated for war trauma out of the 390,000 total casualties of that conflict. So by the start of World War One, if only the evidence had been brought together and noted, there might have been some indication of the reaction that would occur amongst troops, should the war not be over by Christmas.

It was too easy for an Edwardian military man to ignore the numerous instances of 'nervous breakdown' reported in the press when it involved 'unmanly' types like Oscar Wilde, and easier still if the term was used with reference to a woman. Virginia Woolf was later scathing about 'war doctors', most notably when creating the character of Sir William Bradshaw in *Mrs Dalloway*, published in 1925: 'Sir William said he never spoke of "madness"; he called it not having a sense of proportion.' In the eyes of such men, the army had to be a fighting force fit to defend an empire; there was no room for the physically or mentally weak.

Greater emphasis should have been placed on the mental health problems that had already affected young men involved in industrial accidents, particularly as the railways expanded rapidly from the mid-nineteenth century onwards. Initially, those involved in workplace accidents were of little interest to the authorities or the media of the time; it was only when horrific first-hand accounts of railway accidents hit the headlines that newspapers offered more coverage of the after-effects. Many complained of injury following such accidents and the phrase 'railway spine' came to describe the symptoms experienced: largely back pain, but mental health issues too. It is around this time that the first mention of the term 'traumatic neurosis' appears, coined by German physician Hermann Oppenheim to describe such accidents, and investors in the railway companies were concerned that a culture of compensation would develop.

Other doctors, such as eminent French neurologist Jean Martin Charcot, maintained that these cases were only forms of hysteria or neurasthenia, and this lack of consensus may have saved companies from meeting expensive claims. It was not the last time that so-called malingerers were presented as a menace to society before the war.

Dr John Collie, who would later comment on the large number of shell shock victims claiming pensions after the war, gave a long speech to the 1913 London Medical Congress arguing that the authorities needed to take precautions against possible abuses, following the passing of the 1911 National Insurance Act. This was the first piece of legislation to give compensation to those unable to work due to illness, and detractors like Collie argued that it would be abused. Collie claimed that there were undoubtedly a number of long term sick who, 'as a result of introspection which savours of cowardice', would be 'congenitally incapable of appreciating ordinary moral obligations' and would stay on the sickness compensation for longer than necessary. Even 'stolid, respectable working men' – as opposed to those he deemed 'highly strung' – could succumb to the temptation, he contended, especially if encouraged by a ruthless lawyer.

Although such issues were prominent in the media before World War One, the British medical establishment showed no urgency to develop an understanding of the psychological impact of traumatic events. As it was viewed as simply not British and a tad unmanly to break down or become a victim of one's nerves, few doctors thought the subject worthy of research. Ideas of masculine duty and self-control soon had to be reassessed, however, in light of the tragedies of the war, which impacted upon all classes. This military code was vital for discipline, but it would also perpetuate much misery. The 80,000 diagnosed would be a conservative estimate; many more lived the rest of their life with their horrific memories of the war buried deep within them.

'Always they must see these things and hear them'
(Wilfred Owen, 'Mental Cases', 1918)

Many young soldiers went off to war in August 1914, bolstered by the assurance that it would be an adventure, with little thought to long-term risks. Some fresh recruits joined up alongside the professional soldiers, in the hope that it would provide them with employment, warm clothes, boots and hearty meals. Those young men soon realised that, instead of heroism, they must draw on all their endurance and strength just to survive.

The retreat at Mons and the first Battle of the Marne in the late summer of 1914 saw the war quickly turn into a mud-ridden stand-off between armies, using endless bombardment and barbed wire fences rather than hand-to-hand combat. During the retreat at Mons Corporal Bernard John Denore of the 1st Royal Berkshire Regiment, wrote in his diary:

One man was in a very bad way, and kept shrieking out for somebody to bring a razor and cut his throat, and two others died almost immediately.

I was going to move a bundle of hay when someone called out, "Look out, chum. There's a bloke in there." I saw a leg completely severed from its body, and suddenly felt very sick and tired. The German rifle-fire started again and an artillery-man to whom I was talking was shot dead. I was sick then. Nothing much happened during the night, except that one man spent the time kissing a string of rosary beads, and another swore practically the whole night.

No longer was your enemy a visible individual: he was now an idea, a machine, a hidden menace that took away friends and comrades with a bullet or a shell blast. On 2 November 1914, Lieutenant General G.N. Moleworth of the Somerset Light Infantry wrote: 'Another day of hell under the continual hail of shells and bullets. Why have we no artillery to retaliate? Men are being buried alive and blown to pieces all around me. Perhaps death is preferable to this infernal life.'

The first soldiers presenting the symptoms of shell shock were noted as early as September 1914, and many had succumbed within the first 12 months. Books published on the subject offer graphic stories of terror and breakdown, depicting the final crisis capable of bringing a man down and the horrors that so impaired a man's ability to take part in combat that hospitalisation was required, if only for a short period.

Private 'M' was described by Arthur Hurst, a major in the Royal Army Medical Corp and head of the hospital at Seale Hayne in Devon. Hurst records that having joined the army in 1913, 'M' had remained fit until 1915, when his comrades had seen him exhibiting manic behaviour and had prevented him from taking a suicidal leap over the parapet and out of the trench into heavy German shellfire. Hurst recounted: 'He believed he was still in the trenches which were being heavily shelled; his pupils were wide and dilated and he sweated profusely. His pulse was 140. Convulsive tremors of the head, trunk and limbs constantly occurred. In his dreams he saw the ghosts of Germans he had bayoneted coming to take revenge on him.'

We have in mind from dozens of portrayals in film and fiction a picture of an emotionally paralysed young man; eyes staring but unseeing, and deaf to the enquiries of those around him, perhaps. We see him screaming or waking from nightmares so terrible they render him speechless and are repeated, night after night. We hear and read first-hand accounts from diaries or from testimonies recorded by oral historians. It is a litany of despair. But does this represent the true experience of the shell shocked?

The official figure of 80,000 recognised as disabled by the condition after the war (about 2 per cent of those who served), is not truly illustrative of the emotional disturbance experienced by millions of soldiers at the Front. Why did some men appear to end the war without mental scars, whilst others were never to recover? What caused a man to crack? How many were affected, but carried on regardless, only to find that after their return they could no longer function in the society they had come home to?

The Medical Symptoms of Shell Shock

After those first casualties in 1914, numbers of soldiers coming into clearing stations with shattered nerves quickly increased, and it became obvious that many would have to be sent home to military hospitals, which were ill-prepared for men with these symptoms. Physical wounds had been anticipated and provision made for their treatment, but men whose minds were damaged could not find any relief on the same wards as those with bullet wounds or horrific injuries from shell fire.

Some men just needed a break from the shock of their first encounter with mechanised warfare; they could recover behind the line and return to their battalions, more aware of their fragility and better able to manage it. Others were unable to control their bowels, or were in a permanent state of anxiety, and they also exhibited the classic symptoms of shell shock such as losing the ability to speak, or communicating with a marked stammer. Many relived experiences on the battlefield by developing symptoms relating to actions they had taken; tics and uncontrollable facial muscles might be attributed to having bayoneted the enemy in the face, for example. Those who relied on their rifles to maintain their own safety and protect others, such as snipers, might wake up unable to see, while some had shocking nightmares that repeated their experiences over and over again.

As previously mentioned, many attribute the first use of the term 'shell shock' to laboratory psychologist Dr Charles Myers. In his war diaries, published in 1940, Myers said he had not invented the term, but gave no insight as to its origins. He did, however, highlight the symptoms that were becoming more obvious as the first year of the war came to an end: soldiers were 'nervy', emotional, and 'shaky' and experienced tremors, bad dreams and depression.

When Myers first noticed this consistent set of symptoms, he assumed they were as a result of some physical cause, such as proximity to an exploding shell or contact with chemicals. Like others, he considered the possibility that an explosion created a vacuum in the skull and affected the brain, but as he carried out clinical tests, Myers had to conclude that most of the symptoms were not caused by concussion, poisoning or changes in air pressure from a blast. His tests could not find any organic cause, and as ever-increasing numbers of men came in for treatment before they had experienced any shell fire, he realised that the term 'shell shock' was inappropriate. It was too late to prevent it from entering popular discourse, particularly as the phrase offered those affected a diagnosis; it framed the mental experience of war until well after the conflict ended.

In an article published in *The Manchester Guardian* in March 1918, a 'University Correspondent', signing himself 'T H P' (most likely Tom Hatherley Pear, a young psychologist who worked at Maghull Military Hospital) argued that shell shock was one of the 'toughest problems that this war has presented to medical science'. He explained that it was a term now 'admitted into our everyday vocabulary, and has even dropped the apologetic inverted commas which marked the hesitating entrance to the ranks of popular terminology.' 'T H P' felt, however, that it was a pity that shell shock had been so firmly, and so quickly established as a diagnosis because 'the class of troubles and disorders which it connotes is always with us, in war and peace', and 'the toughness of the problem which it now presents to us will not vanish when peace comes'.

More recent commentators have remarked on the obvious class bias that influenced a diagnosis of shell shock. Doctors noticed that officers seemed to experience symptoms of depression, dizziness, palpitations and a feeling of disconnection with the world around them; they had nightmares and complained of insomnia. The men who served under them, however, were described as having exhibited the more physical symptoms of 'hysteria'; they were limping, shaking, blind, deaf and mute. They suffered paralysis of one or more limbs, their muscles contracted and they lost control of bodily functions, were unable to walk, or developed facial tics.

Even those psychologists most sympathetic to the idea that war neurosis did not require a physical cause, who attributed it as a response to trauma and stress, saw the development and classification of the disorder in class terms. In *War-Neurosis and Military Training* (1920), W.H. Rivers wrote:

> One possible cause may be found in difference of general education. On the whole the officer is more widely educated than the private soldier; his mental life is more complex and varied, and he is therefore less likely to be content with the crude solution of the conflict between instinct and duty which is provided by such disabilities as dumbness or the helplessness of a limb.

It was not simply that doctors, who were usually of the same social class as the officers, found it hard to attribute symptoms of what was an essentially 'feminine' hysteria to chaps they might have gone to school with. The way they had been brought up, the ideals of manliness, heroism and the perceived need to stand their ground when all about them were losing their heads, made hysteria impossible to countenance. It smacked of weakness, or cowardice.

Elaine Showalter devotes a whole chapter of her ground-breaking book *The Female Malady* to male hysteria, focusing on the shell shocked man in the Great War. She quotes from an instruction manual for officers in the British Army, published in 1917, which offers a template for an 'ideal' officer. He should be 'well turned out, punctual and cheery, even in adverse circumstances'; he should put his men before himself and be 'blood-thirsty and forever thinking how to kill the enemy'. This vision of heroism was generally impossible to realise in the trenches, where periods of stalemate and boredom were more common than active combat. The proximity of mud, rats and decomposing bodies forced an officer to place his personal appearance and turn out low on his list of priorities.

The War Office became frustrated; more and more soldiers were returning with symptoms of mental distress and a solution eluded those responsible for treating them. Doctors were urged to classify types and treatments and as Wendy Holden details in *Shell Shock*, in theory at least, the classification and treatment regimen was to be unified in the following definitions:

1) Shell shock caused by explosive shock to the central nervous system.
2) Hysteria causing partial or complete loss of control over sensory perceptual motor functions.
3) Neurasthenia, caused by prolonged intense physical or mental strain (including fatigue, headache, exhaustion, lack of appetite).
4) Disordered action of the heart (including palpitations, giddiness and fainting).

The need to classify is benign in itself, but the results were not, as class issues immediately came to the fore. Officers diagnosed as 'neurasthenic' suffered less stigma than the 'hysterical' ordinary soldier. The neurasthenic officer was more likely to be sent home to convalesce in a calm congenial environment, with rest and good food. 'Hysterical' young soldiers experiencing palpitations or fainting spells were often misdiagnosed as physically sick and sent to hospitals without the facilities for neurological patients. Some appeared so badly affected that they were not classified at all and simply consigned to lunatic asylums.

An article in the *Manchester Guardian* of 4 July 1916, illustrates the disparity in the treatment between the classes. Richard Cowan, a young soldier who had joined the Royal Engineers before the outbreak of war, was part of the first British Expeditionary Force, serving through the horrific experiences of the retreat from Mons. In February 1916, Cowan was sent home from the Front, suffering from shell shock and was admitted to Maghull Military Hospital near Liverpool. Following treatment he seemed to improve and his family were keen to care for him at home, or at least to see him settled in a hospital closer to his home in Moss Side, where he could be supported by relatives and friends.

Despite their requests and obvious willingness to take responsibility for him, Cowan was discharged from the army and sent to Prestwich Asylum, where he was classified as a dangerous lunatic. Prestwich was a county asylum, originally built in the mid-nineteenth century to house 400 patients, who at the time were mostly suffering from the symptoms of syphilis, dementia and epilepsy. By the beginning of the twentieth century, an extension to the original building had increased the official capacity to over 1,000, but when Cowan was admitted it was severely overcrowded, housing over 3,000. Between 1917 and 1919 Dr Montagu Lomax was Assistant Medical Officer at Prestwich, and in 1921 he published a book exposing the shocking conditions he had witnessed there. He considered the manner in which patients like Cowan were treated to be 'inhuman'. The building was more like a jail than a hospital and any treatment the patients received seemed only to make their conditions worse.

Richard Cowan's father was horrified. He told *The Guardian* that his son was not 'dangerous' and it would have been quite safe for him to be looked after at home. His protest did not result in his son's release into his care, but the Cowan family refused to give up. After Sir Frederick Milner, an ex-member of Parliament and great supporter of ex-servicemen, became involved, Cowan junior was offered a pension of £1 per week for six months, conditional on his being immediately moved into accommodation set aside for private patients. *The Guardian* reported Mr Cowan's views of his son's treatment in no uncertain terms:

> Mr Cowan, who has three other sons serving in the army, points to the dislike which people of small means have of the Poor Law institution, and especially of the workhouse asylum, and submits that, apart from the indignity which is inflicted upon them, it is a poor return for the services they have rendered their country and the suffering they have undergone if the sons of people who do not happen to have any interest in high quarters are to be treated in the way described.

The same distinction between hysteria and neurasthenia was applied to specific ethnic groups and to foreign soldiers in even more sinister ways. Irishmen and those with southern Mediterranean roots were thought most likely to behave irrationally, while Jewish men were considered equally unreliable. The author of an article in *The Lancet* in 1914 stated that high levels of lunacy in Ireland were a 'legacy of mental weakness dating from the sufferings of the famine years' and after the war Dr Boldie, District Commissioner of Medical Services for 'Ireland (South)' claimed that the high number of Irish ex-servicemen suffering from mental health issues was due to 'a definite Neurasthenic temperament which is prevalent amongst the South Irish'.

These racial stereotypes were reflected in views back on the Home Front, where those panicking during air raids were often described as being 'Jewish in appearance' or 'foreign'; that is, not exhibiting the stoicism of the true Brit. *The Manchester Guardian* (February 1918) reported from an inquest into the deaths of eight people in an air raid on London. The deaths, the court heard, resulted 'from an outbreak of panic which was almost entirely due to persons who might be called foreigners or persons of foreign extraction'. A Superintendent McKay is quoted as saying 'I am proud to say that we have not had the slightest trouble with English people, but we have very great trouble with the foreign element'.

The true nature of shell shock was much more complex and medical men of the time were keen to ensure that only the 'lower classes' were classified with symptoms previously applied to women. 'Mutism', the loss of the power of speech, was almost exclusively confined to soldiers and non-commissioned officers. Elaine Showalter highlights this inability or refusal to speak, when directed at their officers and the military establishment, as a reflection of the same helplessness and frustration some Edwardian women felt towards their situation in society. Their silence certainly affected their treatment both during and after the war.

As the war continued, distinctions were also drawn between the regular or professional soldier, the volunteer and the conscript, called up from 1916 onwards. This may have been prompted by the perceived epidemic of shell shock which arose between July and December 1916, during the Battle of the Somme. In that period around 16,000 cases were recorded amongst British troops, although the nature of that battle must have been the greater problem.

As one survivor, Private Charles Taylor, of the 13th Battalion, Yorks and Lancs, remembered: 'I started crawling towards our lines, and I had never seen so many dead men clumped together. That was all I could see and I thought to myself, "All the world's dead – they're all dead – they're all dead." That's all I could think as I crawled along. Everywhere I passed, to my left and right were dead men laying on the ground.' Corporal Clifford Lane, 1st

Battalion, Hertfordshire Regiment, similarly described his own despair at taking part in battle: 'But there were times, after being shelled for hours on end during the latter part of the Somme battle, that what I wanted was to be blown to bits. Because you knew that if you got wounded, they could never get you away, not under those conditions.'

The view that conscripted men were simply 'not up to it' continued after the war, and in 1922 was taken up by the eugenics movement. In January 1922, neurologist Sir Frederick Mott gave a lecture to the Eugenics Education Society on the subject, 'The neuroses and psychoses in relation to conscription and eugenics'. Mott asserted that there were 'comparatively few' cases of shell shock amongst the regulars, as opposed to the army of conscripts. He maintained that steadfast discipline and morals protected a man from neuroses and that the necessary moral fibre was more likely to have been found in those who had enlisted voluntarily. This is not borne out by the evidence, as men who had volunteered were breaking down within a month of the start of the war, but it is a view that the military establishment would have been happy to promote. Mott also claimed that the war had 'provided no new nervous disease,' and that it was 'the same hysteria and neurasthenia which neurologist knew before the war.'

In the twenty-first century those who work with service personnel recognise that symptoms of post-traumatic stress disorder (PTSD), or combat stress, are very similar to those listed under shell shock in the First World War. They are also symptoms common to many civilians with clinical depression and anxiety disorders. These conditions are not always properly diagnosed, but today most mental health professionals understand that people of all backgrounds and social class can be equally at risk.

Identifying the Cause of Shell Shock

Charles Myers may have been keen to re-evaluate the term shell shock and establish a broader range of causes for the symptoms men exhibited, but others in the medical establishment were reluctant to acknowledge any psychological aspect. They feared that drawing attention to shell shock could damage morale and create a sense of panic, which would result in additional sufferers coming forward. They were also concerned that any recognition of the condition could encourage disaffected soldiers to become 'malingerers', feigning symptoms to escape the front line on sick leave.

As it became clear that officers were suffering disproportionately in relation to the men they commanded (one officer would usually command 30 men, but six times more officers were presenting with the symptoms of shell shock), the establishment began to examine what factors could be causing these young men to break down. Most had been through the public school system and instilled with the ethos of the 'heroic ideal' and notion of duty, that distress should be nobly borne. Ernest Jones, President of the British Psycho-Analytic Association, was convinced that the war had re-written the standards of morality that these young men had been brought up to respect. The sense of fair play, the control of one's baser instincts, was of no use in this new theatre of war. Jones explained:

> All sorts of previously forbidden and hidden impulses, cruel, sadistic, murderous and so on, are stirred to greater activity, and the old intrapsychical conflicts which, according to Freud, are the essential cause of all neurotic disorders, and which had been dealt with before by means of 'repression' of one side of the conflict are now reinforced, and the person is compelled to deal with them afresh under totally different circumstances.

When that shell shocked young man was required to return to civilian life, he could not simply switch off and instead remained on high alert, still functioning at heightened levels of battle efficiency.

Tom Hatherly Pear felt the term 'shell shock' masked many problems that could be compared to the pre-war 'nervous breakdown', a term he also thought inadequate to describe what was happening to those affected. He considered that, far from a man's nerves 'breaking', his ability to react to situations of danger actually increased and became more 'disquieting' as the nervous system grew more sensitive. Symptoms such as 'insomnia, accompanied by and often due to mental excitability, lack of self-confidence, so called obsessive worries, false mental perspective, exaggerated emotional reaction, irritability, hyper sensitivity,' could not merely be the result of something physical 'breaking'.

One hundred years later, veterans of Iraq and Afghanistan complain of the same stresses. Lance Corporal Johnson Beharry, awarded the Victoria Cross for actions in Iraq, has since complained of the lack of support for those in the armed forces on their return to civilian life. Beharry has had his own struggles, and once spoke of his distress at being affected during simple tasks, such as shopping in a supermarket, when a clash of trolleys could put him on battle alert. Major J.O. Langley, author of one of the standard books on shell shock, described symptoms indistinguishable from those experienced by Lance Corporal Beharry. Those who have been trained to kill, and have killed, as Grafton Elliott Smith and Tom Hatherly Pear state in *Shell Shock and its Lessons*, do not suffer neuroses because they have lost their reason, but because their reason and senses were 'functioning with painful efficiency.'

Simply surviving in the trenches exerted unbearable strain on soldiers. Exhaustion set in as sleep became impossible; soldiers witnessed the mutilation and violent deaths of comrades; the subsequent stalemate and sense of futility left them too much time in which to think. For officers, the burden of responsibility was frequently overwhelming. The static nature of the war and the fact that men could neither fight nor flee, created an environment that was against human nature; all the chemicals in the body clamoured to run from a dangerous situation, but duty required otherwise.

Discussions of the causes of shell-shock are frequently framed in ways that were readily understandable to the medical community at the time and resonate now, for a twenty-first century public with a greater understanding of mental health issues. The suffering experienced by Great War combatants is reflected in traumatic events – both in conflict zones and following natural disasters – around the world. There were specific and unique causes of breakdown in trench warfare beyond the sight of dead men, the mud and the sleep deprivation. Perhaps our increased understanding of the psychological effects of trauma is the reason why, 100 years on, the First World War has taken its place as the iconic vision of the horrors and futility of war. Despite the millions of deaths and atrocities committed in conflicts since 1914–1918, it is still the image of the trenches; the endless rows of headstones and fields of poppies that represent 'war' to a British public. The image of the glassy-eyed stare of the speechless, shell shocked soldier still haunts us and defines our fear of madness.

In *The Secret Battle: Emotional Survival in the Great War*, Michael Roper points out that many brilliant historical studies of war trauma mention how 'extreme and sudden horror and fright' could be, for sufferers, the beginning of the condition. We now recognise that involvement in one-off disasters can leave people with similar symptoms, and Roper asks what were the *most* frightening experiences in the Great War, with the greatest potential to traumatise those involved? As mentioned previously, breakdown in battle situations had been identified for centuries before the Great War, so what unique factors within this war created conditions that caused thousands of men lifelong mental pain?

Rather than just a single, devastating incident, for many combatants the need 'to be a man', to repress fear or emotional weakness, was a very significant feature of their breakdown. Officers, who saw their role at the head of a company of soldiers as one resembling a parental responsibility, were especially vulnerable. They needed to ensure the morale of troops did not plummet, even as their fellows were maimed and killed around them, and it was a strain that some could not maintain. Work undertaken more than 30 years after the war, by a man who had experienced this very situation, suggests that this pastoral role was at the heart of the shell shock phenomenon.

Captain Wilfred Ruprecht Bion was born in Mathura, North-Western Provinces, India, and educated in England. At the outbreak of the war he served in the Tank Corps as a tank commander in France, and in 1918 was awarded the Distinguished Service Order (DSO) for his actions at the Battle of Cambrai. In 1918, Bion experienced a moment of intense fear that was to define his life and future career. Whilst moving tanks ready for an attack, as he had done on many previous occasions, he seemed to 'lose his nerve': 'The strain had a very curious effect; I felt that all anxiety had become too much; I felt just like a small child that has had a tearful day and wants to be put to bed by its mother. I felt curiously eased by lying down on the bank by the side of the road, just as if I was lying peacefully in someone's arms.'

This description resonates with twenty-first century psychoanalysis. In the 1950s Wilfred Bion became a leader in that field, and is mentioned alongside Freud as one of the most important voices on the relationship between infants and mothers. Wilfred Bion's daughter, Parthenope, took his work forward and suggested that her father was shaped by his wartime experiences. She was also convinced that traumatised soldiers regressed to childhood when overwhelmed by stress.

Many of us can recall a moment when, faced with an unpleasant task or an event anticipated with terror, we long for someone else to take responsibility, to relieve us of anxiety. Generally, the response is eventually to challenge our fears and learn from the experience. However, at moments of intense shock, trauma or overwhelming emotion, many will retreat to parents or friends for solace. For soldiers in the trenches, even in letters home to the loved ones who would normally have been their first source of comfort, there was an instinct to repress the very worst of their experiences. Aside from censorship by the military authorities, a need to protect those at home from worry, or a simple lack of words to describe the horror, often meant there was no outlet for their fears.

Wilfred Bion, drawing on his own direct wartime experience, described the situation where a man could lose all sense of himself as a soldier in the field and regress to a point where they need not be responsible for controlling fear, seeking childhood again. Even if a soldier, or unit, was coping as a battle raged around them, the sense of relief felt when at last they were given the opportunity to retreat to the comparative safety of the dugout and find sanctuary in sleep is palpable in many letters home. If physical safety was directly threatened, or death close, many soldiers' first instinct was to call for 'mother'. Such an incident was recalled by the late Harry Patch, speaking of his time serving as a private with the Duke of Cornwall's Light Infantry:

> I came across a Cornishman, ripped from shoulder to waist with shrapnel, his stomach on the ground beside him in a pool of blood. As I got to him he said "Shoot me". He was beyond all human aid. Before we could even draw a revolver he had died. He just said "Mother". I will never forget it.

The legacy of this intense emotional experience had a direct effect on those who had remained at home. When sons, husbands and fathers returned after the war, women often felt a new distance in a previously close relationship. They had to learn to appreciate that men had nursed men; that a comrade had taken their place as comforter; and that when they were most needed, in their traditional supportive, domestic role they had not been there. Mabel Lethbridge, a young girl during the war, noticed a distance between those who fought and those who remained at home: 'When my father and brothers, uncles, relatives and friends came home on leave and were staying at or visiting our house, I noticed a strange lack of ability to communicate with us. They couldn't tell us what it was really like.'

For many soldiers, a bond with home was maintained through clothing, from socks knitted by a wife to a trench coat bought by mother – all could become talismans. Poet Wilfred Owen was encouraged to buy a coat by his mother before he left for France. Torn by shrapnel when he was not wearing it, the coat became a way, not only of expressing the closeness of his mother's love, but also the perpetual danger he was in and the blind luck evident in the struggle to survive battle conditions. Those 'certain things' mentioned by Lieutenant Edmund Blundon were often items, thoughts or feelings that were essentially nostalgic, romantic, and ultimately unrealistic, leading to the disappointment many felt after one or two days back home on leave.

Something that reinforces this feeling of retreat to childhood and the home is the iconic figure of the boy-soldier and the idea of an army of young men barely into adulthood. In actuality, the average age of a British soldier during the conflict was early to mid-twenties and in 1914 it was as high as 30, when a greater proportion of those fighting were professional, older men. Wilfred Bion argued that history merely reflects the stress response of the soldier of any age, who could no longer 'contain' his fears. They had insufficient support to maintain their links to the external world and turned inward to unconscious, child-like responses.

This relief from stress was something that the soldier both desired and feared most; Bion called this fear the 'nameless dread' – an anxiety that cannot be identified or made sense of. This explains why so many men, even if they survived the war without obvious physical or mental scars, could still refuse, or find themselves unable to speak of it. Bion himself found it difficult. As psychologists at military hospitals, such as Maghull near Liverpool, saw increasing numbers of men with 'a considerable resemblance to that of a child', their doctors sought a way to relieve their terror and identify the 'nameless dread' haunting them.

It was not only this fear of losing control that haunted soldiers, nor was it simply the build-up of anxiety under unrelenting extreme conditions, made more challenging by lack of sleep and inadequate rations. By 1916, the meat ration per soldier was down to 6oz per day and this was reduced still further until meat was available just one day in nine. A flour shortage resulted in the production of indigestible bread made from turnips. Those cooking for men on the front line had to resort to using any vegetable matter they could get hold of. There were some sights that men found more terrible than others, and deaths that were the stuff of nightmares. Above all, the prospect of a lack of heroism and dignity in death sent many over the edge into breakdown. Comrades were torn apart by shells; a soldier might duck and turn to find the men behind him in fragments, or, like Harry Patch, find a trench in which a man had been disembowelled, still alive and holding his guts, with no hope of survival.

Another torment was a product of the way in which the war was fought. Trenches were significant engineering achievements and they were built to resist collapse. However, a direct hit from a shell could result in men being buried alive along with dead comrades. There was often little hope of digging them out without serious risk to the lives of the rescuers, so they would be entombed until the air ran out. Similarly, the fear of being struck by a shell whilst inside a tank was very real. The occupants would have little chance of escape; once it breached the armour of the vehicle the shell would explode, setting the tank and those inside it alight immediately. Other serious injuries received, even in non-combative circumstances, could lead to the most agonising death. Such an experience is described by Private W. J. Fletcher in his *Memoirs & Letters:* 'Further along the road I saw another tragedy, an infantryman had tried to get onto a moving lorry, a Peerless with exposed driving chains, he must have slipped and caught his leg in the chain. I saw white bone from his thigh to his ankle; everything had been stripped off before the driver knew he was there.'

This fear of being physically torn apart mirrors the experience of mental disintegration. Paul Dubrille, a French Jesuit serving in the Infantry wrote: 'To die from a bullet seems to be nothing; parts of our being remain intact;

but to be dismembered, torn to pieces, reduced to pulp, this is a fear that flesh cannot support. The most solid nerves cannot resist for long.'

The War Office Committee on Shell Shock

On 28 April 1920, a key statement was made by Lord Southborough to his colleagues in the House of Lords. Southborough had tabled a motion, asking for the establishment of a committee to undertake what would now be called a 'root and branch' investigation of the causes of, and treatments offered for, shell shock during and after the Great War.

> The subject of shell shock cannot be referred to with any pleasure. All would desire to forget it – to forget … The roll of insanity, suicide and death; to bury our recollections of the horrible disorder and to keep on the surface nothing but the cherished memory of those who were the victims of this malignity. But my Lords, we cannot do this, because a great number of cases of those who suffer from shell shock and its allied disorders are still upon our hands and they deserve our sympathy and care.

Lord Southborough was born in 1860 and had already spent many years working in senior positions in the civil service, at least one of which was top secret and politically charged. He respected those suffering from war neuroses and could be trusted to organise such an important committee in an impartial and professional manner. He was, therefore, offering himself as the best man for the job, and his colleagues agreed.

The very fact that Lord Southborough had thought the motion appropriate reveals that attitudes amongst those in the establishment towards the possibility of widespread war trauma had changed, even since the Armistice was signed. Public concerns about the large numbers of men who had been court-martialled and imprisoned for desertion or cowardice, alongside the numbers of men still needing treatment years after the end of hostilities, had shaken those in government. The Labour Party was making great political capital of the number of young men shot for cowardice, who should in all likelihood have been treated for shell shock.

Lord Southborough intimates that many would rather have forgotten the horrors of the trenches and the consequences of sending so many young men to face death, disability and madness. Yet, as the aftermath of the war was assessed and the soldiers de-mobbed, few families did not at least know of someone affected by their wartime experiences. For the government, the economic consequences had been huge: new mental hospitals were established; staff received training; and pensions were found for those who could not return to civilian life – all this had depleted the coffers.

In September 1920 Lord Southborough's committee began work; it would not report its findings until June 1922, having examined 59 witnesses. There were 15 members of the committee and the majority had medical expertise. The armed forces were also represented and two members of parliament were also co-opted on to the committee, one a Liberal and one from the Labour party.

The committee was all male, highly conservative and drawn from the middle and upper classes, who were overwhelmingly the product of the British public school system. Only the Labour MP Stephen Walsh, from a working class mining community, could be said to represent the rank and file soldier. However well-meaning, the committee consistently took a patronising and dismissive view of the 'lower orders' and the 'public mind'. Comments reflected much of the recent discussion around racial degeneration and eugenics and still clung to the heroic ideal and pre-war concepts of manliness and character. The medical men generally favoured 'somatic' or bodily theories of mental health, believing that there should be something physically responsible for the symptoms, an organic explanation.

Over more than 18 months, a stream of army officers, regimental commanders, neurologists, psychologists and medical officers with direct experience of treating shell shocked men, both at the Front and back in Britain, appeared as witnesses. Pensions officers were also called, as were soldiers affected by neuroses, although there is only evidence that six servicemen – four officers and two from the other ranks – were heard. Bearing in mind that, in 1920, the committee identified more than 60,000 men drawing disability pensions for mental ill-health associated with the war, and 9,000 still receiving treatment, it seems remarkable now that so few of those directly affected were interviewed.

Despite hearing witnesses with polar opposite views, the eventual report was declared unanimous in its response to both the causes of and the best potential cure for shell shock. Writing in *The Times* in September 1922, Lord Southborough claimed that the committee had believed that they could only submit a report to the army if their conclusions on the meaning of 'emotional disturbance' were unanimous. Historian Ted Bogacz, who has undertaken a close analysis of the findings, contradicts this assertion: 'what may be most striking to the modern reader is the ambivalence, antagonism and even confusion of intelligent men confronted with a startling and ambiguous phenomenon for which little in their background or education had prepared them.'

When the report was published, the newspapers devoted much space to a discussion of its findings, picking up on comments that they perceived would make the best headlines. In truth, the recommendations were insufficient to create any real surprise or excitement. The report maintained that there must be better medical screening at the recruitment stage; that those affected in a mild way should respond quickly to good psychotherapy and, where possible, be treated close to the Front. The name 'shell shock' was to be abolished and soldiers suffering from concussion were to be defined as battle casualties, while those with neuroses were not. Doctors required at least a basic knowledge of 'psycho–therapy' and officers needed to understand the psychology of the soldier. Unit discipline and morale were key (the committee heard that there were far fewer cases in units that were cohesive and stable) and tours of duty should be shorter. 'Frequent rotation and home leave' must be organised and, as far as was possible, good sanitation, comfort and rest were vital in situations where battle strain was likely. The soldier must not at any time be allowed to think that war trauma was an honourable means of leaving their colleagues to fight on without them. None of this advice was revolutionary and in a number of military hospitals more effective treatments had already been found.

Lord Southborough himself took on the responsibility of making the findings public, and phrasing them in terms 'the lay mind' could understand. Firstly, he stressed that 'shell shock' should no longer be applied as a diagnosis to those men experiencing emotional disturbance as a result of the war. He felt it had been a term 'much used and abused' and 'born of the necessity for finding at the moment some designation thought to be suitable for the number of cases of fundamental nervous incapacity which were continually occurring among the fighting units.' Some men had been diagnosed with shell shock to avoid the stigma that would otherwise have been attached to a diagnosis of a mental disorder unrelated to their war service.

Having taken out of the equation 'commotional disturbance' (i.e. being directly affected by an explosion, leading to a concussion and hearing loss, for example), Lord Southborough turned to the bulk of the report, which dealt with 'emotional disturbance'. It was, the committee decided, of two types. The first was more readily understood by members of the public – a 'nervous breakdown' due, Southborough said, to: 'strain and hardship, fatigue, inadequate rest, loss of sleep, wet and cold, misery and monotony, unsavoury cooking, nauseating environment, mud and blood.' When the army was moving forward and seemed to be making progress, cases were far fewer, and this type of breakdown was 'nervous exhaustion' rather than 'neurosis'; a man's body ceasing to function, rather than losing his nerve. That loss of nerve was 'emotional disturbance', the subject of the last, and most disputed, section of the report dealing with the large number of shell shock cases attributable to 'loss of control of the mind or nervous system'.

It was at this point that Lord Southborough first mentioned cowardice, ensuring that readers of *The Times* understood it to be a crime, punishable by death. The public was now familiar with the stories of those shot for desertion or cowardice, many of whom had been young, and previously brave, young men. The report was not going to pardon them; instead, it concluded that in many cases of shell shock, the men had only themselves to blame. With a mere nod to poor recruitment practices and public demand that every physically fit man able to hold a gun should 'do his bit', Lord Southborough quotes a 'well-known doctor' as having given giving the following evidence:

A tremendous number of neurotics resented having been passed, and they had never the slightest intention of trying to make soldiers of themselves. An enormous proportion had been neurotics previously ...
A large number of fellows broke down long before they had finished

their training ... They knew they could never stand the long marches and they never intended to.

The doctor's uncompromising testimony was chosen for publication in the national press and, in the eyes of the public, it immediately branded this 'enormous' ' tremendous' and 'large' number of men as cowards with no thought to duty and the defence of their country. Other parts of the report attributed blame to poor discipline in some (unnamed) battalions, but the officer class was largely unaccountable for the large number of soldiers breaking down. It was the rank and file soldier, the poorly trained volunteer, the inadequate conscript who appeared, to the committee, to be at the root of the problem.

In 1916, 21–year-old Private Arthur Sidney Addison was sent out of a trench on the Western Front, accompanied by another soldier, to collect a seriously wounded man and carry him back on a stretcher. The two men ploughed their way through the mud, while under fire. On the way back, as Arthur Addison was walking at the head of the stretcher with the other man behind him, both straining to hold their man, the party was hit by the blast from a shell. The wounded man and Arthur's comrade were instantly blown away and, in shock, Arthur Addison ran and hid in a shell-hole until someone came to find him. Trembling and terrified, he found not sympathy but fury, and an officer swiftly arrested him for deserting his post. Mercifully, the court martial was more understanding and he was acquitted and sent back to the Front. Eventually discharged from the army as unfit, a victim of mustard gas and sniper fire resulting in the loss of his right testicle, Arthur was always to suffer nightmares and remained petrified of thunderstorms all his life. Not a regular soldier, but a young, previously fit apprentice gas fitter, he was a working class volunteer of whom the committee's report was prepared to believe the worst.

The overwhelming sense one gets from reading the report is that despite an acknowledgement that shell shock could affect anyone, in truth only the 'inferior' break down. It is, they considered, the working class, the lower ranks who have fallen victim to this hysteria. In *Forgotten Lunatics of the Great War*, Peter Barham calls this 'putting Tommy Atkins in his place.' Even into the 1920s, as the report was being compiled, more and more ex-soldiers were finding themselves incarcerated alongside civilians classified as 'insane'. Most would have come from the lower classes; some were poor and already malnourished, unfit for the rigours of the trenches.

The publicity surrounding the report did do much to highlight how far British society needed to shift to ensure that any future war was not conducted in the same way, with the same results. By 1930, encouraged by the report's findings, the Labour Party saw the successful result of a long campaign to end the death penalty for cowardice, despite continued opposition in Parliament. If there is a positive message to come out of a report riven with class bias, racial prejudice, stereotyping and misunderstandings of the true nature of mental ill-health, it is the acceptance that no soldier was exempt from the effects of war trauma. The Eton-educated may suffer from neurasthenia rather than the hysteria of the man from a working class family, but both could break down.

The 1922 *Report of the War Office Committee of Enquiry into Shell-Shock* was described by Bogacz as an 'iconic document', which had 'increased public awareness in the 1920s of mental illness and of the new psychology of Freud and other theorists of the unconscious.' It was certainly progressive in its adoption of elements of Freud's vocabulary, even if it repudiated his theories, but had genuine progress been made? Post-First World War Britain was still a long way from understanding what made some men break down in the face of an ordeal that others could leave behind them on the battlefield.

Chapter Three

Science, Shrinks, Trickcyclists & Nutpickers

During all wars in the twentieth century, doctors of the mind were sent to assess, manage and treat men whose nerves had gone. Throughout the First World War, the emotional distress of the patients they were faced with could be overwhelming for many physicians. With little real experience of such trauma and few effective treatments to draw upon, doctors could not balance the needs of their patients with those of their paymasters; their real role was to get a man fit for battle once more. Rarely could they avoid experiencing the guilt of sending a trembling young man back to the Front, or a sense of helplessness, as experimental treatment after experimental treatment failed. Repression versus catharsis, discipline versus indulgence; it took many years and more than one conflict for the medical establishment to draw properly researched conclusions. Still into the twenty-first century, there are as many opinions as there are doctors.

The Great War saw the beginning of academic study into the concept of war as a psychological, as well as physical experience. Doctors, especially those working in psychiatric medicine, wrote copiously of their experiences with individual patients and of their opinions on treatments. However, apart from Charles Myers, who served with the Royal Army Medical Corps, many psychologists had no front line experience; they had been safely back at base, or practising on home soil. In Britain military psychiatry has been, until recently, very much neglected. After each major conflict, from World War One to the wars in Iraq, peacetime returned the doctors to other specialities and the urgency subsided.

More recently and particularly as anniversaries and the commemoration of conflicts approach, historical and medical academic inquiry has once more increased. There has also been a call for greater understanding of the stresses experienced by those servicemen and women engaged on what are now, at least nominally, called peace-keeping missions. The most recent deployment, of service personnel in Afghanistan, has once more highlighted the mental health issues soldiers face. With no excuse for ignorance in the twenty-first century, many consider there is still insufficient understanding within the medical profession and society as a whole. As Ben Shephard points out in *War of Nerves – Soldiers and Psychiatrists 1914–1994,* and as confirmed during my own research for this book, much of the existing historical research work focuses on race, gender and the emotional impact of the Great War on modern memory. Doctors who chose to focus on the shell shock victim as 'malingerer' and 'coward' are rightly vilified.

However, it is also clear that not to acknowledge the fact that *some* young soldiers may have taken an opportunity to escape or enjoy a break behind the lines, would be as singular an omission as to avoid mentioning the young men and women who actively benefited from their period in the armed services. Many others coped with the horrors and later emerged to employment, marriage, and rewarding, comfortable lives. When mental health professionals still cannot definitively answer the question of who is most vulnerable to breakdown, what can we conclude was learnt by doctors treating shell shocked soldiers? What findings went on to inform the diagnosis and treatment of mental ill health in the general population after the war?

The depiction of the military and medical establishments offered by contemporary writers, such as Pat Barker in the *Regeneration* trilogy and Sebastian Faulks in *Birdsong,* and the war poets and novelists of the early twentieth century can be misleading. War poets and authors had their own agendas and biases, even if they were empathetic and angry about the lack of understanding of the reality of war in the civilian population.

In mythologising the victims of shell shock we let them, and those still fighting for their country, down. In *War of Nerves* Ben Shephard comments, 'It is becoming increasingly clear that doctors of the PTSD generation have gone through the same learning process as the World War One doctors. Indeed there appears to be a recurring cycle with war neuroses; the problem is first denied, then exaggerated and finally forgotten.'

During the first years of the war, treating those unfit for battle but presenting with no physical symptoms was difficult. The army was not prepared for the number of casualties, and places in specialist hospitals were few and generally reserved for higher ranking officers. Even officers could find themselves in the care of non-specialist general practitioners, or doctors who focused on unmasking a 'malingerer', rather than assisting the genuinely ill. A few were prepared to take an alternative view, yet they were still under pressure to fulfil the military requirement: they had to get men back to the Front.

Shocks, Psychotherapy and Phospherine: 'Curing' Shell Shocked Soldiers

Remarkable Testimony!

The following remarkable testimony – entirely unsolicited – is but one more tribute to the marvellous restorative powers of Hall's Wine.

Original letter on file:

"I had a gruelling time in France and Flanders, as a result – suffering from acute shell-shock – I lay at the Base lacking both speech and memory. In the end the trouble developed into a distressing form of neurasthenia. Four months in hospitals wrought but slight improvement and the doctors agreed that I would be of no further use in the Army, or indeed civil life. During convalescence and pending discharge I took Hall's Wine with really remarkable results. Weakness gave place to strength, trembling to steadiness. To the astonishment of everyone I am again buoyantly 'doing my bit'."

Stored in every bottle of Hall's Wine is just that strong reserve of energy and vigour which we all need in times like the present.

(Advert placed in the local and national press by Stephen Smith & Co. Ltd. September 1917)

Hall's Wine was not the only product advertised as a cure for those suffering from shell shock or any manner of 'nervous' complaints. Whatever ingredients were in Hall's Wine, Dr Cassell's Tablets, Phosferine or other patent medicine available from a chemist, wine merchant or dubious sounding private addresses, they were unlikely to have cured shell shock (or deafness, kidney problems, sleeplessness, indigestion or any number of other annoying complaints).

This section will look at the various treatments employed to 'cure' shell shock within members of the armed forces, as well as examining three of the major military hospitals and preparations taken by those at home during and after the war. Whether wounded in body or mind, the military authorities were keen to ensure men were treated quickly and returned to fight the enemy as soon as possible. This treatment was seen as part of the military machine and, on the whole, men remained with fellow service personnel and were nursed by voluntary aid nurses (VADs) trained to deal with the horrific injuries of war. Many wounded men remembered the great kindness shown by medical staff and it also added to their sense of kinship with fellow patients and perhaps moral superiority over often insensitive civilians. Others found the process was rather less positive, and the experiences of men affected by shell shock were compounded by the uniform soldiers convalescing back in Britain were required to wear.

'Convalescent' or 'hospital blues' were adopted as an efficient and cheap way to ensure a high standard of cleanliness within military hospitals. A man arriving muddied and bloodied in boots, greatcoat and well-worn uniform required stripping and bathing; his clothes needed disinfecting too, as they may have been lice-ridden and torn. It was far better to supply him with something cheap and easy to wash for the duration of his stay. Blues consisted of ill-fitting jacket and trousers made of flannel and flannelette, rather like ugly pyjamas, and were worn with a shirt and red neck-tie. They were available in general sizes but shrank in the wash; their appearance was not designed to make a man feel good about himself, particularly in comparison to the khaki uniform, which to many was a symbol of pride. The figure of the injured soldier in blue elicited much respect and sympathy, and was used to great effect to raise funds by charitable organisations, such as St Dunstan's. Some men found the heroic associations of the blues were also attractive to women. However, the uniform could be used to make an injured man a figure of fun; he became the subject of cartoons and postcards.

In the films of shell shocked soldiers made in 1917 at Seale Hayne Hospital (described in greater detail later in this chapter), the men look institutionalised in their blues. The trouser legs are short, the jackets tight and the overall impression is of discomfort rather than pride. To a modern eye it is obvious that each man has been stripped of his individual identity. The uniform, worn as it often was with an armband indicating the stage of recovery reached, seems designed for the benefit of the institution rather than that of the patient. Key, important features were forgotten.

In civilian wear by then men wore trousers and jackets with numerous pockets, ensuring that money and valuables could be kept about their person. Women's garments did not usually include pockets, and so they used handbags to carry everything they needed. The design of soldiers' blues lacked pockets, assuming that in hospital the wearer would not require money or train tickets, for example. In a sketch by J. Peplow, published in the *Journal of the King's Lancashire Military Convalescent Hospital* in 1917, two men in blues are seen walking with small bags, one in what was then considered an effeminate manner. The sketch is subtitled 'Owing to the shortage of pockets in the wearing apparel of the convalescents it has been suggested that they should copy the ladies and carry handbags.' Gender roles were highly significant in the aftermath of the war, and anything, even the most minor alteration of dress, challenged a man's view of his place in society and could affect his self-esteem on his return to civilian life.

Approaches to Treatment – Medicine or Psychotherapy?

When the moon hangs red in the darkened sky
There's a shadow in grey who comes to my side
He is Fear, he said
As he sat at my head
And he gazes deep, though I fain would sleep,
When the moon hangs red in the darkened sky
There is terror abroad
In the darkened ward
And the sleepers moan, as they toss and groan,
While in their dreams run
The sound of the gun
But the watching shadow of shapeless grey
Hovers around till the break of day.

('The Terror', Roy Bishop, undated)

The experience depicted by the author of this poem was not uncommon among those receiving hospital treatment for the psychological effects of the war. Men came home from the Front to find that the treatment they received was determined by the hospital they were allocated to, rather than individual clinical need. Some were also experimented upon in the name of cure. Electric shocks, trickery, dubious drug treatments and different approaches to psychotherapy were all used with what appeared to be some success, in the short term at least. The sheer numbers being treated made it hard for largely inexperienced medical teams to consider men as individuals but, as with the uniform of convalescent blues, institutionalisation was often the only way to keep the system moving.

The treatment plan given in hospital usually proceeded as follows:

1) Each patient on admission to have a hot drink
2) Each patient to have three full meals a day unless otherwise ordered
3) Do not discuss the symptoms with the patient
4) No-one is permitted in these wards unless assigned for duty
5) The rapid cure of these patients depends on food, sleep, exercise and the hopeful attitude of those who come in contact with them

This list, applied to each patient regardless of individual need, might be supplemented with a rest cure (usually restricted to officers) or a period of solitude. Doctors might also prescribe a restricted diet, usually unpleasantly milky or including such delights as the 'Beef Tea Custard' detailed in a British Red Cross recipe book for volunteer nurses:

Required: Two or three eggs to each pint beef tea. Sugar to taste.

Method: Strain the beef tea well before using or a heavy sediment falls to the bottom of the dish. Beat the eggs, add beef tea and beat again, well strain into buttered dish and bake 20 to 30 minutes. Custards must be baked very slowly. The pie-dish may be stood in a baking tin of water, which helps to set them firmly by preventing too quick a heat from reaching them.

There was no cohesive position across the medical establishment as to the best way to approach what we would now call an individual care plan. Homogeneity was often the only way a hospital could manage the volume of patients being admitted and symptoms were grouped together and treated in sometimes conflicting ways. It was difficult to maintain a hopeful attitude whilst enduring what effectively amounted to solitary confinement. Psychotherapy, as a discipline, was then in its infancy and treated with scepticism by doctors who believed shell shock to be neurological rather than psychological in origin. There was also a reaction against the Victorian approach to the treatment of generalised neurosis, which largely involved the prescription of increasing quantities of laudanum, leading to addiction, life-threatening side effects and overdose.

However the First World War did offer a new intervention for shell shock, designed to ensure men stayed as close to the fighting as possible. P.I.E., or rather proximity to battle, immediacy of treatment and expectation of recovery, was first implemented by the French army and adopted by the British Expeditionary Force in 1916. Field hospitals were inundated with men suffering from the stress of battle and instead of sending them back to the safety of a hospital miles from the Front, they were treated in centres within earshot of the fighting. They were offered rest, hot food and graduated exercise to return them to fitness, and to the trenches. This forward psychiatry was based on a 'bank balance hypothesis', acknowledging that a man had a finite amount of fortitude and if he was taken too close to mental bankruptcy, breakdown would result.

Statistics from these hospitals seemed impressive, with up to 80 per cent of admissions returned to their units. But a significant bias in reporting must be acknowledged; if some success could not be shown, what was the use of having psychiatrists at the Front at all? Reliance on these statistics resulted in P.I.E. being utilised in the armed forces until the late twentieth century, when in fact most men treated in the hospitals were only fit for support roles, and others were returned to the trenches to break down for a second time. Then there was no going back, and a man would be on a ship back home to a hospital in Blighty.

Approaches in hospitals back in England varied widely but did, however, influence the ways in which mental health was treated post-war and developed the treatments that underpin those still used today. Below, the different approaches are examined, each of which had consequences for post-war mental health treatment.

Lewis Yealland and Faradization at The Queens Hospital

Although electric shock treatment was used at other military hospitals during the war, it was taken up as a crusade by Canadian-born neurologist Lewis Yealland, who worked out of The National Hospital for the Paralysed and Epileptic, Queens Square, in London. Yealland was convinced that shell shock as a disease did not exist and that men who were unable to speak or paralysed in one or more limbs simply needed reminding of their duty. If they continued to be unresponsive, he believed they should be encouraged to acknowledge that duty, through a treatment involving the application of increasing levels of electric current to the affected parts of the body, even the larynx.

Yealland is credited as one of the doctors most successful in returning even the worst affected men to the field of battle, although how many of the frequent relapses he was responsible for is impossible to say. His treatment is shown in its full horror in the film of Pat Barker's *Regeneration* trilogy, in which Yealland appears to torture a mute man by placing electrodes in his mouth and shocking him until we hear the beginnings of garbled speech. Not so cruel as depicted in the film, Yealland was, nonetheless, one of the doctors least sympathetic to the cause of the traumatised service man.

Yealland co-wrote a paper called 'The Treatment of some common war neuroses' for *The Lancet* in 1917. Within it the authors suggested that their patients (usually ill-educated rank and file volunteers and conscripted soldiers) were weak-willed and determined not to respond. Therefore, rather than offer the months of psychotherapy that other, more empathic doctors might prescribe (though usually to officers) they preferred to experiment on those young men with 'faradization'. This agonising treatment was intended to convince the patients that simply by putting their minds to it they could get better. If a man resisted, electrodes would administer short but increasingly powerful and painful electric shocks. At the first signs of recovery the patient would endure an unremitting regime of 'command and persuasion' (always with the threat of further electric shocks in the background), until he submitted to the doctor's will and changed his behaviour.

In *War of Nerves*, Ben Shephard describes Yealland as 'fervent, sincere, over-dramatic … not just a doctor in action but an evangelist grappling with evil, driving the devils from the patient's body'. To a twenty-first century reader, familiar with stories of human rights abuses, this seems like little more than sadism. The focus is on the removal of physical symptoms, rather than the underlying trauma that is their cause. Faradization was a battle of will between doctors and their patients, in which the doctors had the most effective weapons.

The use of electric shock treatment developed significantly throughout the twentieth century. It is not Yealland's direct legacy, but patients still dread the treatment, which, as 'electro-convulsive therapy' or ECT, is now used as a last resort in cases of major depressive disorders and schizophrenia.

Maghull Military Hospital and W.H. Rivers at Craiglockhart

A very different approach to that of Yealland was taken at Maghull Military Hospital, just north of Liverpool. The institution was originally built as a centre for the treatment of epileptics, but as it was still without patients when war broke out, the War Office reassigned it to the treatment of less seriously affected shell shocked men. A bed at Maghull was a world away from staying in an old, decrepit asylum and the staff were also of a more progressive and reforming attitude; some went on to take the treatments they developed at Maghull to other hospitals. William H.H. Rivers, the psychiatrist who treated Siegfried Sassoon, famously worked as an RAMC captain at Craiglockhart War Hospital near Edinburgh, where he developed the psychotherapeutic approach he first used at Maghull.

Maghull Hospital quickly filled up with casualties, but it was critically short of staff until a temporary appointment was made, which also determined the direction the hospital would take in its treatment of the psychologically damaged soldier. Dr R.G. Rows, the former assistant medical officer and pathologist at Lancaster County Asylum, was given the role of medical superintendent at Maghull in July 1915. Calling upon the expertise of Professor Grafton Elliot Smith, Dean of the medical school of Manchester University, the hospital was staffed with other gifted men, such as lecturer and psychologist Pear, whose writings on the treatment of shell shock are still referred to today. With William Rivers, the team worked to make Maghull a hospital that was considered a centre of excellence.

Unlike Yealland at Queen's Square and Frederick Mott at the Maudsley Hospital, Maghull focused on psychological medicine as a means of identifying the causes of war neuroses. As the men admitted were not suffering from serious forms of psychosis, these war-damaged soldiers were involved in informal experiments into new ways of managing mental illness. Along with important neurological clinics like the Maudsley, treatments pioneered at Maghull were hugely influential post-war.

Grafton Elliot Smith and Tom Hatherly Pear wrote an influential book late in the war, entitled *Shell Shock and its Lessons*. In it Grafton Smith maintained that, far from being hereditary, shell shock and 'psychoneurosis' could happen to anyone, if circumstances were difficult enough. He commented:

A psychoneurosis may be produced in almost anyone if only his environment be made 'difficult' enough for him. It has warned us that the pessimistic, helpless appeal to heredity so common in the case of insanity must [be abandoned] ... In the causation of the psychoneuroses, heredity undoubtedly counts, but social and material environment count infinitely more.

William Rivers at Craiglockhart

Craiglockhart had originally been built as a hydropathic clinic, offering wealthy clients the opportunity to take the water cure in grand surroundings just outside Edinburgh. When William Rivers arrived to take up his post as senior psychiatrist, he found an environment in which soldiers were encouraged to be optimistic, cheerful and active. Snooker and billiards, tennis and croquet encouraged a social atmosphere in stark contrast, as Siegfried Sassoon pointed out during his stay there, to the lonely and terrifying nights in which men relived the events that had caused their neuroses.

Rivers was keen to use the work of Freud, but was not a supporter of the theory that neurosis could always be traced back to a sexual response. He did, however, use Freud's theories of repression and the interaction of the conscious and unconscious mind. His success as a therapist lay in his belief that far from forgetting or repressing the memories of horrors experienced on the field of battle, as many well-meaning souls recommended, it was vital to talk openly about the experience and address the grief soldiers were feeling. For many, the treatment was just what they needed to work through the loss of friends, or deal with the events they had witnessed in a more positive way. For others the cure was partial, providing at least some respite from dreams filled with terrible images, and for the remainder there was no route to peace of mind through therapy. One case Rivers reported is quoted in Shephard's *War of Nerves*:

> [*a young officer*] was flung down by the explosion of a shell so that his face struck the distended abdomen of a German several days dead, the impact of the fall rupturing the swollen corpse. Before he lost consciousness, the patient had clearly realised his situation and knew that the substance which filled his mouth and produced the most horrible sensations of taste and smell was derived from the decomposed entrails of an enemy.

For this man's treatment Rivers could only recommend the peace and quiet of the countryside, where the damaged man had previously found a little solace.

The fame of William Rivers is in part due to Siegfried Sassoon, who was treated as a shell shock case by him at Craiglockhart, after having denounced the war and narrowly avoided court martial. Sassoon may never have suffered the true symptoms of shell shock, but he was an eloquent witness to the suffering of the men at Craiglockhart, including his fellow poet Wilfred Owen. Rivers' legacy was to give Freudian techniques of psychoanalysis a platform upon which others could build. Whether or not more conservative authorities liked, it Rivers' 'talking therapy' was successful and has been used in various ways by different branches of psychotherapy ever since.

Frederick Mott at the Maudsley Hospital

The Maudsley Hospital on Denmark Hill in London was initially established before 1914 as a research-oriented institution, designed to take in voluntary patients exhibiting the symptoms of mental ill-health. However, it was not completed until 1916 when it quickly became a specialist treatment centre for non-wounded cases of neurasthenia and mild psychosis, under the leadership of Major Frederick Mott.

Mott approached shell shock from a physiological, rather than psychological, perspective. He saw the emotional symptoms as secondary to the physical ones, in opposition to the position taken at Maghull, but he did acknowledge that even the strongest man could succumb, a bombardment acting as the final straw to a man already under a 'severe nervous strain and fearful apprehension'. He concluded that some men were predisposed to neurasthenia due to an inherited or acquired condition and produced statistics that suggested 74 per cent of the men he treated for shell shock had a family history of mental illness, in comparison to 10 per cent of men who exhibited physical wounds.

Where the Maghull treatment regime was relaxed and informal, the Maudsley maintained military discipline, requiring patients to stand to attention and salute an officer when he arrived on the ward. Mott was not convinced by the claims of psychotherapy and believed there were few doctors with the skill to use it properly. His treatments were based on quiet, rest and distraction, offering simple occupations such as knitting and basket making (hence the term 'basket cases'), although he was not averse to using electric shock treatments and suggestion to 'trick' a man into recovery: 'I have cured functionally paralysed hands…by telling patients that their hands are cold and benumbed and the blood supply to the part is insufficient to excite the nerves…but after it has been warmed by radiant heat they will be conscious of it and be able to move the fingers.'

Mott's treatments are not detailed but he aimed to soothe and to relax the men, offering numerous warm baths to cure insomnia and encourage restorative sleep. However, like the doctors at Maghull, he was keen to stress the importance of training and research and saw the value of work undertaken with shell shocked soldiers for the larger concerns of psychological medicine.

Arthur Hurst and Seale Hayne Hospital

If you visit the Wellcome Collection in London (or its website) you can view some disturbing footage of men apparently in the most desperate stages of shell shock, exhibiting their symptoms for the camera. Later, there are more scenes showing that some of these men have undergone a quite miraculous recovery. Entitled *War Neurosis 1917*, the film was shot over a period of eight months at the Royal Victoria Hospital at Netley, near Southampton, and at Seale Hayne Hospital, near Newton Abbot in Devon. It is the only surviving footage of the effect of shell shock on British soldiers in the Great War.

Major Arthur Hurst, who had volunteered for service with the Royal Army Medical Corps, was as qualified as many of those who worked to cure traumatised men during and after the Great War. Having established a neurology department at Guy's Hospital in London, he travelled to France to see the work doctors there were doing with men diagnosed as suffering from hysteria. Hurst also saw the horrors of war first-hand in Gallipoli, before coming back to England to put his learning and theories into practice.

Having obtained a grant from the Medical Research Committee to make the films, Hurst directed them himself, using skilled Pathé cameramen at both hospitals. As a doctor he wanted to highlight his work with traumatised patients, many of whom had been unsuccessfully treated under the care of other eminent medical men. At the time, Seale Hayne was offering treatment unavailable elsewhere and when released in 1918 the films led to Hurst being lauded as a miracle worker. However, other doctors treating neurasthenia were less enthusiastic, considering Hurst a self-publicist whose methods were impossible to verify.

Even 100 years on, the 'before' and 'after' shots are fascinating. Patients were initially filmed at The Royal Victoria Hospital at Netley, built on Southampton Water after the Crimean War and, at the time of the film, the army's principal military treatment centre. Hurst then moved his team, along with 100 patients, from Netley to Seale Hayne in April 1918. Seale Hayne was originally established by the Right Honourable Charles Seale-Hayne, a wealthy local landowner who bequeathed £100,000 for the establishment of a 'college for agricultural and technical education near Newton Abbot'. Before the building of the college was completed, war broke out and it was offered to the War Office, first used to train members of the

Women's Land Army until Hurst spotted the opportunity to commandeer a secluded and under-used building as a base for his work. Seale Hayne was officially requisitioned for use as a military hospital until late 1919. A beautiful creeper-clad building, it can still be visited and is now owned by the Dame Hannah Rogers Trust.

Hurst's film, whilst ostensibly offering a tool for training other clinical staff, is a masterpiece of promotion and marketing. One can watch it as a piece of social history, but as documentary evidence of medical treatment it is exploitative and disturbing. Footage of a small number of young men is represented as evidence of the efficacy of Hurst's shell shock treatment plan. Among the men filmed was Private Percy Meek, a 23-year-old from Norfolk, who joined the army in 1913. First wounded in the thigh in May 1915, he was treated and returned to the Front later that year and served without further incident until February 1916. Hurst's lengthy report on Meek's case explains that the young man was stationed in a trench subjected to a period of continuous bombardment by German mortars. As the noise and anxiety became overwhelming, Meek's comrades had to prevent him from going over the top in panic, to attack the German position.

When first examined by doctors Meek was dazed and confused, experiencing exhausting convulsions which caused the constant movement of his head, body and limbs. Mute, but still able to understand questions put to him and write a response, it became clear to doctors that Meek believed he was still in the trench, breaking out in a sweat as imaginary shells hurtled by him. Transferred to hospital in England he remained unable to speak, his expression was fearful, and he saw the ghosts of Germans he had killed coming towards him, firing, bent on revenge.

When Arthur Hurst first met Meek the young man had already been in hospital for some months and his condition had steadily worsened, leading to paralysis in his arms and legs, which were rigid and numb. Hurst reports that limited use of electric shock treatment to his larynx enabled him to whisper, but it became clear he had no memory of events, nor did he recall his family and friends. In *War Neurosis 1917*, we first meet Meek at Netley, captioned as a 'complete retrograde amnesia, hysterical paralysis, contractives, mutism and universal anaesthesia'. We see him sitting like a baby, in a straight-backed, wooden wheelchair, undergoing an examination of his rigid ankles for the benefit of the camera. Yet over a period of months his voice and understanding gradually returned, and, after transferring to Seale Hayne in April 1918, his physical recovery quickened and the film shows a much healthier looking Private Meek, wearing the uniform hospital blues and running up and down the steps in front of the building. The film shows his recovery to be so nearly perfect that by June 1918 we see him supervising fellow patients in a basket weaving shop at the hospital.

In the film we see other young men exhibiting a range of symptoms. Private Preston, aged 19, reacts to the word 'bombs' by leaping under his hospital bed, while Private Ross Smith, aged 35, has a facial spasm affecting his ears and head with violent twitches, which disappear under hypnosis, only to return with renewed violence when he wakes. Private Reid, aged 32, was buried by debris from an exploding shell and, though without physical wounds, he has become unable to move; the film shows him returned to full mobility and able to work on the hospital farm.

In another section of the film we see Privates King and Sandall, captioned (in Hurst's unique term) 'hysterical stump orators'. Both blown up in 1917, we see them in January 1918, walking up and down the pavements of Netley, rolling with a 'hysterical' gait and speaking to each other in an animated and unnatural way. Hurst notes that Sandall imitates King and goes on to describe how, with just two hours of 'treatment by suggestion', the symptoms were removed. Both men are sent to work on the hospital farm, but the film highlights King's 'incompetency at digging', which results in him, appropriately as a former bookseller, being made hospital librarian.

The simple peace of the rolling Devon countryside offered solace to the damaged men. Physical activity – working on the land, tending cattle – was an important part of the therapy and Hurst even encouraged men to re-enact the battles they had been involved in, equipped with firearms. Creativity was encouraged and the men produced a lively magazine, complete with hospital gossip column. In between these activities, Hurst and his team also offered lengthy and intense sessions involving hypnotherapy and what was termed 'humane persuasion'. Unlike some other hospitals, the staff at Seale Hayne refused to bully a patient into submitting to the will of the doctor and the army. Hurst was keen to ensure the dignity of the men was maintained, with no pressure to get them back to the Front at all costs.

In evaluating Arthur Hurst's treatment, it would be easy to compare his methods to twenty-first century approaches to treating depression and anxiety. To the frustration of his peers, Hurst was always evasive when answering more technical questions about how his results were achieved. In the film, he describes the soldier's symptoms on screen but he does not elaborate on the treatments. He tells of how visitors to the hospital were often surprised at the rapidity of his results, but mentioned little other than the fact that men were 'kept at it' for hours until the treatment was successful. His isolation from other experts in the field, such as Frederick Mott, Charles Myers and the doctors at Maghull and Netley Military Hospitals, meant that few came to witness work in progress, and the remote location of Seale Hayne negated the possibility that anyone else could take credit for his successes.

It was not until 1944, when publishing an updated version of his book *Medical Diseases of the War*, that Hurst detailed his methods:

> Directly the patient is admitted the sister encourages him to believe that he will be cured as soon as the doctor has time to see him…The medical officer … tells him as a matter of course he will be cured the next day. The patient is made to understand that any treatment he has already received has prepared the way, so that nothing now remains but a properly directed effort on his part for a complete recovery to take place.

It appears that Hurst was simply tricking his patient into recovery. Deception was widely used as a 'cure' for shell shock and it was not considered an unethical practice. Fake operations to cure deafness were staged, the staff going so far as to anaesthetise and cut patients who had been told the procedure would cure them. Frederick Mott at the Maudsley Hospital also used fakery, alongside 'Faradization', or electric shock treatment. In addition to his distinguished work as a neurologist, and his understanding of the fight or flight reflex, he recognised that, as the war progressed towards a conclusion, and men sent back to the Front were relapsing at such a high rate, the best 'cure' was to assure a patient that they would never be sent back; a factor that may have contributed to Hurst's success later on in the war.

It is hard to assess which parts of Hurst's film are what would now be termed a reconstruction and which are genuine. The facts of Private Meek's trauma are undisputed, but the film, shot in just eight months, documents a recovery that took over two years. Presumably the wheelchair scene and Meek's paralysis must be faked or the time frame could not fit. Demonstrations of the disappearance of Private Smith's facial tic under hypnosis are so extraordinary as to be unbelievable and there is little doubt that Privates Sandall and King are playing to the camera and imitating their former 'hysterical gait'. The film is moving and disturbing, but inevitably one begins to doubt the veracity of what one is seeing as there was no requirement, as there is today, for a documentary film to make it clear that a scene is being 're-enacted'. Audiences, still unused to seeing moving pictures would have taken them at face value.

Whether one accepts such fakery as a means to an end ('suggestion' was the term used, but we might compare it to twenty-first century neuro-linguistic programming), other criticisms can be levelled at Hurst and many other doctors who, even though given funding to do so, failed to undertake any follow-up reporting. The non-existent tracking of patients after they left the hospital – either back into the army or civilian life – means there are no statistics to indicate success rates. Hurst was widely criticised for making claims for rapid cures that he was unable to substantiate even six months after the war, let alone years later. The relapse rates at the Front suggest that many men returned after treatment were in no fit state for combat, either psychologically or physically. The long term impact of shell shock on post-war society was almost certainly, in part at least, a result of ineffective treatment in the first instance.

In March 1919, *The Sunday Times* and local press printed lengthy excerpts from an article by Mr W.S. London, Honorary Secretary to the Middlesex War Pensions Committee, written following his visit to Seale Hayne Hospital. The article, headed 'Modern Miracles', describes how 'the dumb are made to speak, the deaf to hear, the blind to see and the paralysed to walk.' The papers held Mr London up as a paragon of honesty, noting that he 'only speaks of what he has really seen with own eyes, so that there can be no question of exaggeration!'

Knowing now that fakery and re-enactment were fundamental tools in Dr Hurst's medical bag, the descriptions of a paralysed and dumb man being 'cured' within 10 minutes, to the point where, simply by coughing, he can be encouraged to sing the whole of 'It's a long way to Tipperary', appear somewhat suspicious. The end of the article offers interesting statistics; within five months of the end of the war, Hurst and his team could claim that in 100 consecutive, successful treatments, they were curing, within days, men who had on average been treated in other hospitals for 11 months prior to admission. Ninety-six per cent were treated and cured in just one sitting, at an average of 54 minutes per patient. Of the four cases that required longer, all took less than four weeks. Despite these claims, without statistics it is almost impossible to establish what percentage of the men treated later relapsed.

Some aspects of his techniques are now recognised as effective in the treatment of depression and anxiety. Physical exercise and fresh air have been shown to reduce anxiety and lift mood, and there is little doubt that the support Hurst and his staff offered to those desperately afraid to return to the Front aided recovery. However, hypnotherapy and suggestion, which Hurst used to 'cure' patients very quickly, is disputed as a treatment for more serious mental health issues.

Such follow-up studies have been difficult to carry out in subsequent conflicts. In a BBC Panorama Special screened in the United Kingdom in July 2013, the subject of suicide amongst veterans of conflicts from 2000 onwards (particularly those serving in Afghanistan) showed a continuing dearth of follow-up data. This lack of information was blamed for a rise in the number of ex-servicemen taking their own lives, having experienced the onset of the symptoms of post-traumatic stress disorder either during or years after their tours of duty. It is an issue the Ministry of Defence, the National Health Service and society still need to address.

Models of Mental Health Treatment – a Post-War Legacy?

Despite the differences in approach, the military hospitals and doctors treating traumatised men left a legacy for the inter-war treatment of those with continuing, mental health problems and for the general population. In 1917, the battles of Arras, Messines and Passchendaele flooded hospitals with casualties, resulting in the return from France of Charles Myers. He established a three-month training course in psychological theory and practice at Maghull, to ensure doctors would be better able to identify and treat the symptoms of trauma even after the war.

The training and research undertaken at the Maudsley Hospital resulted in a post-graduate qualification for asylum doctors and, despite the success of many of the doctors trained at Maghull, it was the Maudsley that became the medical model. Hospitals such as the Tavistock Clinic and Cassel Hospital tried to maintain the profile of psychological therapies, but with government funding cut, they struggled to offer support to any but the wealthiest patients.

After the Armistice, there was an effort to reduce the stigma of mental illness by creating 29 outpatients clinics to support men back into employment. But many men were abandoned, seriously mentally ill, in county asylums, their symptoms untreated. In Peter Barham's words they became 'the forgotten lunatics of the Great War.'

Self-help and Miraculous Recovery

Regardless of the success, or otherwise, of the various treatments adopted by doctors, there remained a remarkably buoyant market for the patent medicines frequently advertised in the press, and an enthusiasm for stories of so-called miracle cures. Desperate to believe that those men coming home from war with shattered nerves could somehow be cured, the public lapped up the column inches devoted to the subject in national and local papers.

Before the advent of the National Health Service, many British families approached chemists or took what would now be considered quack remedies, rather than involve a qualified general practitioner who might charge fees beyond a working class family's purse. In the advert for Hall's Wine reproduced at the start of this chapter, the makers claim that a soldier, about to be discharged as unfit for both army and civilian life, had found nowhere else to turn other than the wine merchant. It seems unlikely – and the letter may indeed be bogus – but many young men were left in this position. Dr

Cassell's tablets apparently gave similar relief, as did Phosferine, according to a newspaper advert of 1916 which offered this testimonial from one R. L. Kearns, a former private from the King's Liverpool Regiment:

> I feel that I must write a few words in praise of your wonderful preparation 'Phosferine' and let you know how grateful I feel for the effect produced by it in my particular case. I went to France in November 1916 and engaged in a great number of scraps with the Hun, until I was returned to England in March 1917, suffering from shell-shock. You can imagine what Winter is like in the trenches, and especially to one who was never very strong.

Kearns goes on to mention that, as he had seen others benefit from the tonic, he gave it a go and found that it soon 'had the effect of bringing about a complete reversal in my condition', making him stronger than ever before. The makers of Phosferine proudly state, 'this war-battered soldier knows that only by the aid of Phosferine has he been able to overcome shell-shock', and they proceeded to offer a special price to service personnel who would benefit from the tonic. Available 'from all chemists', Phosferine was also described as an effective cure for anything from sciatica to lassitude, brain fog to indigestion and maternity weakness, and even recommended for children. It was sold well into the 1970s and the National Archives holds a number of papers suggesting that this tonic, as well as Dr Cassell's Tablets and other miracle pills were licensed by Beechams.

A little research reveals that Phosferine is still available as a herbal supplement. Now obliged to list its ingredients, rather than the phosphoric acid it used to contain (the same chemical that gives coca cola its brown colour), its active component is cinchona bark, and it is recommended, amongst other things, for haemorrhoids and increasing the appetite.

If these patent medicines failed to work, then there was always the hope of spontaneous recovery, stories of which inevitably made the papers. For example, in September 1916 *The Evening Telegraph and Post* reported that Private Tolcher of the Royal Irish Fusiliers was diagnosed with shell shock and unable to speak. Then, at the beginning of the 1917/18 football season he attended a football match between Millwall and West Ham United –

always a fixture full of incident. Tolcher suddenly 'recovered his power of speech' at a particularly exciting period of play.

The same paper told of Private McNulty of the Royal Inniskillen Fusiliers, who had been through a number of treatments for shell shock, including electric shock treatment. He was discharged from Netley Military Hospital when all treatments had failed, and while he was travelling home to Belfast by boat from Liverpool, 'a bundle of iron rods was dropped' into the hold 'with a great clatter'. Apparently, McNulty was surprised into an exclamation, after which he 'immediately started to practice speaking'. Another man was 'cured' after being knocked down by a car and another when he accidentally put the lighted end of a cigarette in his mouth. These cases suggest that a sudden start or shock was the basis of the 'cure', something Lewis Yealland would have agreed with, although none of these events were associated with a punishment regime or a battle of wills.

The papers also published a number of ideas that, at first glance, look flippant and silly, but which are now quite often recognised as suitable treatments for those experiencing mild to moderate depression or anxiety. In 1919, the *Courier* reported the 'wonderful results' of a new treatment for shell-shock: swimming. The 'highest' medical authorities agreed that 'constant swimming is one of the best known cures for what may be called shell-shock paralysis'. 'Scores' of servicemen were being treated with swimming regimes in the top military hospitals and 'wonderful cures' had been effected for those who had lost the use of arms or legs. Swimming is a great therapy for those disabled both physically or mentally by war, being low impact and relatively relaxing, and physical exercise of any kind is now known to raise mood and reduce stress.

Some politicians were cynical of the claims made by so–called therapists, or helpful well-wishers. In April 1919 *The Guardian* reported a discussion in the House of Lords in which Lord Knutsford commented that many 'absurd and extraordinary suggestions' for cures were misrepresenting their value to men still suffering eight months after the end of the war. He was particularly critical of a woman who had suggested to him that patients may be treated by playing the guitar. Therapists in the twenty-first century frequently consider music as therapy, to positive effect in some cases, but Lord Knutsford was scathing, saying that the method had 'already been tried when David played before Saul'. Similarly, he dismissed other claims that 'neurasthenia was a gas' and that there was a patent remedy for 'stopping the leakage', as well as the idea that men should be encouraged to live naked in the woods to 'enjoy the morning dew'.

Neither of these ideas made it into regular use, but Lord Knutsford's cynicism aside, his point was a good one: everyone thought they had a cure for shell shock. In the decade after the war even the best doctors in the country were still working through their ideas and some believed that no single 'cure' was any better than another, as long as a man recovered.

One of the most interesting and least known treatments was that adopted by the Maudsley Hospital in 1918, when several wards were painted in 'special Kemp Prossor' colours for shell-shock and neurasthenia. The material used was 'Benger's Matone', which Prossor, an academic, claimed was made to his specification in special registered colours. Howard Kemp Prossor was interested in the impact of the use of colour in the design and decoration of buildings. He developed a palette which he believed would have a curative effect if used on wards in which neurasthenic men were treated. However, he was only given the opportunity to test his theory late on in the war in the Maudsley and a small number of other hospitals around the country.

Prossor worked to the principle that a combination of colours 'should be used which suggest to the mind "Spring", the time of life and recuperation.' Believing colour to have a similar effect on the nervous system to music, an ability to soothe or to energise for example, he also thought the level of each colour in a room was important. Rooms in each hospital were painted in a combination of colours representing and encouraging a sense of 'life': yellow signified light and sunshine, blue the sky, and green plant life.

Prossor claimed a number of successes. Patients, he stated, attributed improvements in their health not only to the colour itself but to the smell of the paint. In the twenty-first century a number of counsellors, psychologists and complementary therapists attach an importance to colours; green is considered restful and calming, for example and in marketing, blue is seen as powerful and professional.

Although little follow up research was done to assess the Prossor effect, there is sufficient modern evidence to suggest he may have had a point. Similarly, even though the adverts for the other, non-medical, dubious, 'cures' have disappeared, there remains a belief in the use of homeopathic and herbal remedies, such as valerian and St John's Wort, for the treatment of anxiety and depression. Mental illness – from mild anxiety to clinical depression and psychosis – requires a wide range of treatments; no one method suits every patient.

Chapter Four

The Heroic Ideal & the Superfluous Woman

W hat does it mean to be a man? A century on from the beginning of World War One, the discussion continues; and the gulf between what societies perceive to be gender roles and what individuals experience seems as wide as ever. The evolution of traditional family structures is under way and has moved on apace even since the beginning of the new millennium.

Imagine then, the position of men and women living in Britain at the outbreak of war in 1914. Historians from both sides of the conflict have agreed that the summer of 1914 was one that would never be forgotten. German physician Magnus Hirschfeld wrote: 'It was an outbreak of madness which raged through the streets at that time, an explosion such as had already been experienced and described, but which had never been fanned into such a world-burning flame'.

Both men and women remembered living through these days with an intensity rare for those who may have been conditioned by a repressive Victorian upbringing. Across Europe cities were alive with pent up excitement and fear as war became inevitable. Like many anticipated horrors, it came almost as a relief to know exactly what must be faced. Communities came together and even the more restrained villages, towns and cities of Britain were enlivened by the possibility of conflict. 'Even when we try to rationalise the matter we are left with the feeling that reason had very little to do with it,' commented politician and writer W. Maxwell Aitken.

Part of this response had its roots in the relationships between men and women during the pre-war period. Women had gained greater, if still limited, educational opportunities and some were working in male-dominated professions during the first decade of the twentieth century, but the traditional roles of protector and breadwinner still belonged to men and those of home-maker and child-raiser to women. On the outbreak of war, men leapt to protect everything dear to them, national and domestic, in response to propaganda, such as 'The Women of Britain Say 'Go'!' Right would win out over the might of the German war machine, and the war would be over by Christmas. Bill Haine V.C., an officer in the 1st Bn Honourable Artillery Company said in an interview in 1973:

> Well, I thought the same as everybody else. Everybody said, "It'll be over by Christmas and you've got to get out soon, otherwise you won't see anything." But I don't know if it was my opinion, or if everybody was saying it. One certainly changed one's mind when we found how well-organised Jerry was compared with us for instance. And how thinly we were on the ground, of course.

We know much about the movement for women's suffrage and the lengths to which activists would go to highlight inequalities in a society that still assumed a woman's role to be a domestic one. Historians have explored how the Great War offered women a chance to prove themselves in the workplace and gave them opportunities that they could build on after the war, albeit with constant challenges. Less is understood about the role of men and how their view of what constituted manliness was affected by the war. Pre-war certainties were challenged by the ways in which men responded to life in wartime and post-war Britain. The period between 1914 and 1918 resulted in a real shift in the way society defined the differing roles of men and women. In a sense, the war highlighted the lack of equality not just in practical terms for women, but in emotional terms for men as they struggled to express their feelings openly.

At first, the British military authorities approached the war with the confident zeal of an imperial nation; the enemy, armed with machines rather than moral right, would be defeated by heroism and the belief in a code of honour and virtue. As stalemate settled across the fields of France and Belgium, it became clear that, to win, Britain would have to meet might with similar firepower. The moral code that the professional soldier took into the war was immediately in doubt, as it became clear that new ways of killing would prevail. The mental health of those in the firing line would raise basic questions about the origins of mental illness and particularly how it manifested in men.

Historians have examined how Victorian and Edwardian ideals of imperial manliness trickled down through society, so that in 1914 more than 40 per cent of adolescent males were in a youth organisation of one form or another. The most influential organisations were the Boy Scouts and the Boys' Brigade, which promoted self-control and command of emotion as necessary qualities for anyone called upon to do their national duty. Robert Baden Powell, founder of the Scout movement said that 'happiness is not mere pleasure, not the outcome of wealth. It is the result of active work rather than passive enjoyment of pleasure' and 'the Scoutmaster teaches boys to play the game by doing so himself'. Such statements reinforced the sense that young men of all classes must step up and play the game.

Being 'morally good' was not enough, a man was also required to have a strong physical presence, demonstrable athleticism and an ability to set aside his own fears for the good of his fellows and his country. The lessons taught by these organisations were more about repression than expression; this doctrine stripped men of individual identity and stressed a heroism that for many was impossible to live up to.

As the war progressed, old prejudices towards male mental illness were challenged. Breaking down was not, as many thought, a matter of education, family or ethnic background. Official figures show that one third of all medical discharges were for a 'nervous disorder'. Many of these patients were officers, brave, well-trained men, who had often been decorated for valour in the earlier months of the war. This was hard for many in the establishment to accept; if breakdown could not be countered by a public school education or strict military training how could anyone prevent it?

What made this random and unpredictable mental trauma more difficult to accept was the challenge it presented to the idea of manliness. Officers, like Robert Lindsay Mackay of the 11th Battalion of the Argyll and Sutherland Highlanders, felt the need to present an impenetrable image to their men. Lindsay recalled one instance showing the gap between his appearance and real feelings in his diaries:

Macleod, the adjutant, turned to me tonight in the Orderly Room and told me that Sergeant McQuarrie of 'D' Coy, who was in my R.A.M.C. party had come up to him, on behalf of the men of the party to ask him to tell the C.O. how well I had done or something or other in the way of work during these barrages. Felt very bucked at such a thing coming so spontaneously from the men, though it is all nonsense, for I 'had the wind up' all the time.

Officers knew that, to retain their position of authority and to inspire confidence, they must never show fear, despite the fact that they were far more likely to be killed or seriously injured than other ranks. They were responsible for the men under them as well as their own safety and courage was all about the capacity to remain in control. For those responsible for taking the country to war – politicians, senior officers, medical men – it was important to find some explanation when an officer's courage failed, which could also be used to sift out other potential threats. Those with the potential to break down must therefore be identified and excluded from positions of responsibility. Distinctions were chiefly based on the theory of eugenics, racism and social prejudice. The southern Irish man was thought to be particularly weak-willed, owing to a perceived Irish predisposition to insanity apparently identified well before the war. To many in the British military authorities, shell shock threatened not only morale amongst the troops, but society as a whole.

These prejudiced theories may have dominated the consideration of insanity among British military authorities, but they were coming up against challenges from abroad in the early twentieth century. European psychoanalysts were examining what it meant to be human, regardless of gender boundaries. The idea of the unconscious mind and the battle with conscious actions would frequently make the front pages of the press during the war. As the numbers of dead increased and the war dragged on, it would have been natural for those who were coping with loss or caring for loved ones changed forever, to have asked questions about what had really happened to their relatives and why. The war challenged the confidence of a nation, requiring many to accept personal tragedy for a national objective that was becoming less clear as the war dragged on. Sigmund Freud summed up the possible result of this bewilderment: 'Neurosis is the inability to tolerate ambiguity'.

'It made me what I am' – Living on after the Armistice

For many ex-soldiers and their families, nothing changed after the war. Men came home, resumed their pre-war lives and continued relationships with their families which were, on the surface, perfectly functional. Many working class households continued to have a main male breadwinner, with perhaps the wife and older children also earning. If a wife had taken on war work, after 1918 there was a backlash against married women working. This letter from the Carlisle Trades Council and Labour Party to a local employer is indicative of the stance taken by many local authorities:

> During a discussion at the last meeting of my General Committee, in connection with the unemployment question, it was alleged by one or two of the delegates that the Liquor Control Board were continuing to employ married women whose husbands were in receipt of a living wage, and I was requested to bring the matter to your notice. My Committee feel that, at a time like the present when there are such large numbers of men and women unable to obtain a livelihood, an effort should be made to do everything possible to absorb those who are now practically destitute as a result of the government decision to withdraw the Out of Work Donation.

In 1914, before the outbreak of war 3,777,000 women were working; by 1918 that figure had risen to 4,936,000. However, the introduction of the Pre-War Practices Act in 1918 required employers to offer jobs then held by women to returning servicemen and that, along with the reduced demand for munitions work, left three quarters of a million women without work.

The return to apparently unaltered pre-war domesticity was a common experience. Yet, there is little doubt that many veterans of the conflict found the transition difficult, feeling themselves changed and displaced. After years of comradeship in the trenches, their abiding memory of the war was often one of community with fellow combatants and initiation into a club or society. That club excluded all those who, by virtue of age, gender or infirmity, had no experience of the horrors of the Front and it could separate veterans from the community they lived in.

Many gave off an aura of endless disenchantment, anger or resentment, and sought each other's company and a sense of shared, if silent, understanding. Others were bombastic, drawing attention to their difference, assuming superiority over those who had not fought and desperately clinging to the heroic role of combatant. However they might seek to convince themselves that life had returned to normal, they were still on some level experiencing a chronic and unhealthy grief.

Literature of the post-war era has framed memories and perceptions of the conflict throughout the past century. Books featuring shell shocked soldiers, such as Virginia Woolf's *Mrs Dalloway* or Rebecca West's *The Return of the Soldier*, have shaped the way we think of the men who returned to civilian life. Most present them as damaged and unable to re-establish relationships with loved ones and the world around them, while some described the situation of shell shocked veterans of the war more generally in their work. In *The Unpleasantness at the Bellona Club*, published in 1928, Dorothy L. Sayers vividly brings the sense of emasculation men felt on returning home to life, as part of an essentially light-hearted crime story. Sayers shows her detective protagonist, Lord Peter Wimsey, a man with his own war story, in conversation with a suspect, who was a young soldier:

"And how are things going with you?" he [*Lord Peter*] asked.

"Oh rotten as usual. Tummy all wrong and no money. What's the damn good of it Wimsey? A man goes and fights for his country, gets his inside gassed out and loses his job, and all they give him is the privilege of marching past the cenotaph once a year and paying four shillings in the pound income tax. Sheila's queer too – overwork, poor girl. It's pretty damnable for a man to have to live on his wife's earnings isn't it? I can't help it, Wimsey. I go sick and have to chuck jobs up. Money – I never thought of money before the war, but I swear nowadays I'd commit any damned crime to get hold of a decent income.

For many ex-soldiers, the powerlessness they felt in the face of the enemy continued in the post-war era, as employment eluded them and relationships with wives and children became strained.

The Superfluous Woman

Ghosts crying down the vistas of the years,
Recalling words
Whose echoes long have died,
And kind moss grown
Over the sharp and blood-bespattered stones
Which cut our feet upon the ancient ways.
But who will look for my coming?

Long busy days where many meet and part;
Crowded aside
Remembered hours of hope;
And city streets
Grown dark and hot with eager multitudes
Hurrying homeward whither respite waits.
But who will seek me at nightfall?

Light fading where the chimneys cut the sky;
Footsteps that pass,
Nor tarry at my door.
And far away,
Behind the row of crosses, shadows black
Stretch out long arms before the smouldering sun.
But who will give me my children?

('The Superfluous Woman', Vera Brittain, 1920)

The role of women in the Great War and the long-term impact the war had on their lives is the source of continuing research. A century on, myths are still being over-turned as academics in the field of women's history tease out the truth. The war accelerated social change and the process of female emancipation in two key areas: marriage and work. In terms of their mental health, the medical and psychiatric research undertaken to support the troops returning with shell shock also changed the ways in which women were treated for psychiatric disorders.

Women were essential to the war effort, and were instrumental in the rebuilding of Britain during the twenties and thirties, yet for many years the 'surplus' female has stood as a symbol of wasted womanhood in the post-war period. The Great War was responsible for the deaths of some 700,000 men from Britain alone, the majority of whom were young, previously fit and, if unmarried, almost certainly in the market for a wife. Their loss left thousands of single and widowed women. As Vera Brittain suggests in her melancholy poem above, many felt that their options were now more limited and that perhaps they must accept spinsterhood as their lot.

In *Singled Out*, Virginia Nicholson focuses on the 'two million' unmarried British women across all age groups, as indicated by the 1921 census. This figure is rounded up from the census data, which in fact shows the number to be nearer to 1.75 million. Analysis of the census only partly supports her view of a post-war generation of women destined for a single life, showing a large gap in the 25–34 age group, where 1,158,000 women remained unmarried as opposed to 919,000 men.

However, the situation is more complex and the gender imbalance was not entirely due to the war. Issues were often class and age based, rather than universal. Professor Jay Winter has argued that the war actually increased the popularity of marriage, though women born between 1894 and 1902 were less likely to find a partner than earlier or later generations. In 1932 the Registrar General published figures showing that in 1919 and 1920 the marriage rate was 30 per cent higher than the pre-war rate, and re-marriage by widows increased by 50 per cent. In relative terms though, a higher number of officers were killed than the lower ranks, and therefore the cohort of upper and middle class women in their mid-twenties to early thirties just after the war were disproportionately more likely to struggle to find a husband.

In February 1920, Dr Murray Leslie gave a lecture to the London Institute of Hygiene in which he expressed 'grave concerns' regarding what he perceived to be a disturbing imbalance between the sexes. *The Daily Mail* reported on his lecture at length, under the headline 'A million women too many – 1920 husband hunt'. Leslie saw a serious threat to social stability: women were becoming discontented; they had greater freedom and were given too much room for sexual licence by neglectful parents. The state of marriage was collapsing, owing to male infidelity, although the blame was attributed to the large number of unattached women available to tempt them – the 'Jazzing flappers' in revealing outfits who fought like cats over spoiled young men. Daughters of respectable households were forced by economic circumstance to go out to work. Only the 'lower orders' were left to re-populate the nation, and in Leslie's eyes, as Virginia Nicholson puts it, 'the country was going to the dogs'.

The public response to the speech was telling. Women wrote to newspaper agony aunts in melancholy tones of their own difficulties in attracting the few men to go round; 'Competition is keen' and 'my chances do not seem very bright'. Women also felt they had to dress more provocatively in order to attract the choosy male, and there was no sign of a new equality in relationships in these tales of blighted hopes.

When the initial results of the 1921 census became available, the press made much of the fact that women far out-numbered men under alarmist headlines. There were more measured articles, such as an editorial piece in *The Times* which made it clear that the disparity was 'by no means attributable to the war alone'. Looking over previous census data the paper highlighted a continuing trend: in 1831 there were 1,040 women to 1,000 men; in 1871 it was 1,054 to 1,000; in 1911 1,068 to 1,000 and in 1921 the figure had increased to 1,095.

As the paper points out, the war had accentuated, but not caused, the gender imbalance. In 1851 30 per cent of women aged between 20 and 40 remained unmarried, and by 1891 the figure was almost a third of women aged between 25 and 35. Infant mortality had long been higher amongst boys and there was also a steady decline in the birth rate from the late Victorian period to the start of the war. The trend continued and a new one emerged – marriage was being delayed, only slightly, but enough to cause concern amongst those who saw a declining birth rate as a threat to the defence of the British Empire.

Rosemary Wall has worked extensively with the Overseas Nursing Association (ONA) and, in recently published research she discusses the ways in which British authorities tried to redress the post-war gender imbalance. As mass emigration became a feature of the late Victorian period and first decade of the twentieth century, it was clear that approximately two thirds of those leaving Britain for opportunities elsewhere were men. Working class women and distressed gentlewomen had been encouraged to seek a new life overseas from the mid-1880s, when the British Women's Emigration Association helped women to find a passage overseas. This was an attempt to redress the imbalance between the sexes in British colonies throughout Africa, Canada, Australia and New Zealand.

In 1919 a dedicated committee was formed to promote female emigration. The Society for the Overseas Settlement of British Women was funded by the government and intended not simply to provide marriageable females to the Dominions, but also to send women over to work in useful professions, as nurses, in agriculture and in training. This was done in spite of the fact that the casualties amongst service personnel from the Dominions Royal were so high that the Empire could no longer provide better marriage prospects than back home in Blighty. As Rosemary Wall points out, these attempts at re-balancing the figures were thwarted by the continued enthusiasm for emigration amongst men; in 1920, 125,000 women emigrated, but then 115,000 men also left to seek a brighter future.

Of course, not all women sought fulfilment solely through marriage. This focus on the necessity of marriage to make a woman's life complete denies the realities many married women faced both before and after the war. Middle and upper class wives in Victorian and Edwardian society had limited career opportunities and narrow social contacts. Endless leisure grew stultifying. As Virginia Woolf wrote her eponymous heroine, 'Mrs Dalloway is always giving parties to cover the silence.'

For women below the poverty line, any romantic notion of marriage would be quickly cast off, as they endured multiple pregnancies and undertook menial jobs to supplement their husband's low income. Yet, in all walks of life, just after the First World War the notion that a woman's place was in the home seemed too long a tradition to cast off.

Having watched their mothers and elder sisters struggle, some young women decided that the answer to potential marital unhappiness and domestic difficulties was not to get married at all. Florence Nightingale, who eschewed marriage to pursue her vocation, was a heroine to many women, and by 1913 more than 60 per cent of the Women's Social and Political Union members (run by the Pankhursts) were spinsters. Those who had never felt the urge to take on marriage and motherhood could, in post-war society, at last find other ways to express themselves, supported by new property laws, improved health care and birth control.

In post-Great War Britain, the doom-mongering warnings of Dr Murray Leslie and his ilk were already being disregarded. After women had taken on more active roles in their communities during wartime, and had time to reflect on the absence of a husband or father, the balance of power within relationships began to evolve. Many couples had married quickly as war approached, in case the worst happened but for some the 'worst' turned out to be the marriage itself. Others found that the injuries loved ones returned with were too much to endure, or would deprive them of the opportunity to have children. Separation and divorce were no longer impossible. On the outbreak of war, it was possible for those on low incomes (having less than £50 per annum or for women less than £2 a week) to be granted the services of a solicitor and counsel at no cost, except the expenses of solicitor and witnesses. In 1914 88 divorces were obtained in this way, at an average cost of £10. By the time most men had been demobilised, about 40 per cent of divorces were obtained using this procedure. Even at the usual cost of around £50 to £60, divorce rates trebled in the year after the war, but for most couples divorce was still not an option; for working class couples it was too expensive and those in the upper echelons of society risked social ostracism.

In the first half of the twentieth century it was not easy for most women to articulate the need for a physical expression of love, those few belonging to middle class 'Bohemian' sets which freely discussed the intimacies of their sex lives, were the exception. The work of D. H. Lawrence is alive with female desire, but other writers of the inter-war period, such as Elizabeth Goudge and Freya Stark, knew their audience well enough to realise that these were not considered fit subjects for respectable young women to read about. Goudge, a deeply intelligent and religious woman, had herself suffered a nervous breakdown after a particularly fraught period in her life. Other writers sought to express the dangers of sexual passion in their novels. In *The Rector's Daughter*, published in 1924, Flora Mayor's heroine is a clergyman's daughter and spinster doing good work in her local parish. Suffering an unrequited love she tries to quell the dangerous, sexual feelings she experiences and has to deny.

In Radclyffe Hall's novel *The Well of Loneliness*, published in 1928, the subject of sexual feeling between two women shocked Britain at a time when open lesbianism elicited hostility and the risk of being labelled a sexual deviant. *The Sunday Express* reviewer stated 'I would rather give a healthy boy or girl a phial of prussic acid than this novel', but in artistic communities the book was ridiculed as superficial and Vita Sackville West considered it 'loathsome'. It remains a classic lesbian novel and despite its reception in the press and some literary circles it must surely have offered comfort to women struggling with their sexuality in its depiction of the 1920s.

In the world outside the novel there is little written evidence of a sense of sexual frustration among unmarried women, but a letter from a Miss G.E. to Marie Stopes, the author of *Married Love*, dated May 1926, offers a glimpse of the repression many exercised:

> Can you help me any in the matter of the unmarried problem? … I am a Gospel preacher; I am President of a Mission. Aberdeen teems with girls. I love them – they know it and feel it. I seek to lead them to Christ. I enter into their difficulties all I can. If they care to give me their confidence I honour it, but never force it. Very naturally sex, love and emotion is one of the biggest. They may love someone else; they may love me! I prefer them to, to loving someone worse who might unscrupulously play on their tender feelings. I respect those feelings and honour the body. I a little bit understand the suffering of repressed nature and sympathise instead … Oh! The struggles! I do not mean, to keep pure; but because they are pure and have no intention of being anything else … but the struggle with life and sex-nature within is an agony …

Miss G.E. is expressing her own struggles as well as those of her girls. The support of friends and the love of parents and siblings could not always have made up for the physical closeness of a loving partner, which many craved. As Virginia Nicholson states in *Singled Out*, '"she never married …" represents a warning sign inscribed with the phrase DON'T ASK'.

'Women Wanted Urgently': Working for the War Effort

The war had not only accelerated changes in sexual and marital relationships for women, but had also offered professional openings and freedoms which some were reluctant to relinquish after the Armistice. For them, marriage was not the only way to achieve long-term security. Working for a living was no longer the mark of the impoverished; it had become a badge of honour. How dispiriting it must have been for those who were expected to make way for the returning troops, keen to take up their pre-war employment once more. Around 750,000 women were made redundant in 1918 alone.

Ray Strachey, feminist historian and editor of *Our Freedom*, published in 1936, commented on the suffragist's view of working women: 'Work, indeed, came to seem almost an end to itself to some of them and they attached a value to earning their own livings which that somewhat dreary necessity does not in reality possess.'

Of course, many of the jobs assigned to the 1,600,000 women during the period 1914–1918 were difficult and dangerous. Working in a munitions factory, as 950,000 women did by the time the Armistice was signed, was liable to create long-term health problems. The munitionettes working with TNT became known as 'canary girls', as the lengthy contact with sulphur found in TNT caused jaundice and consequent yellowing of the skin. Explosions and firearms accidents put them in constant danger and they knew their lives were at risk. In January 1917, for example, the Brunner Mond factory at Silvertown in the East End of London was the site of a huge explosion that killed 69 workers and injured 400 more. Eyewitness accounts to bear witness to a horror, press reports of which were unable to escape the censors.

While propaganda posters of the day show attractive young women, smiling as they did their bit for the war, the reality was rather different. Women worked long hours in poorly ventilated factories, and those with children would have tucked them up at night in clothes covered with noxious chemicals. The argument that war work offered women financial independence is weighed against the fact that they invariably received lower wages than male workers doing comparable jobs. They had to supplement the family income whilst the men in their families were away at the Front on reduced pay and the armament industry made huge profits at their expense.

Despite this, Gail Braybon, author of *Out of the Cage: Women's Experiences in Two World Wars*, maintained that many women found their factory work exciting and even 'liberating', offering them the opportunity to feel part of the war effort. Many left domestic service, voluntarily or because of the increasing cutbacks necessary in middle-class households, to work in better-paid factory jobs, earning as much as £5 per week in the most dangerous occupations. But factory owners and other employers often blocked any moves that might have ensured that women received a fair wage equal to the men they replaced. They took on more women at lower rates of pay – perhaps breaking a skilled role into multiple, less skilled elements to refute any suggestion that a woman had directly replaced a male worker.

Some women had cleaner, although not necessarily safer, jobs in government departments. Others took the places of men on the buses to keep the public transport network moving; a few were drivers, but more than 2,000 women, including Alfred Hardiman's sister Bessie, worked as conductresses, or 'Clippies', issuing and checking tickets. Many women also took on heavy duties in the Women's Land Army.

The financial rewards of the availability of war work are far more often discussed than its psychological impact. As more women went to work, there was a recognised liberating effect: independence, improvement in financial circumstances; a widening of a social circle outside the home and family and a feeling of doing their bit for the war. There was also a new respect for their talents, recognition that, whatever their menfolk might think, they were capable of more than cooking, cleaning and child-rearing. It was a boost to self-esteem and a means of dispersing the unspoken melancholy, loneliness and grief felt by many women for the period of the war. It was also seen as a morally healthy option by social campaigners who lobbied for useful, supervised work to be provided for young women who lived in towns that were rapidly becoming centres for barracks and troop movements. 'Little imagination is needed to picture the evils that may arise when a girl in a state of mental restlessness produced by the war finds herself unemployed with much free time on her hands,' *The Times* quoted from a reader's letter in 1914.

When the war finally ended – and with it many women's jobs – the Restoration of Pre-War Practices Act forced many women back into domesticity. Many had contracts fixed for the term of the war, while others were made redundant to make room for men returning from the services. Some women had been offered valuable childcare as an inducement to work, but found it withdrawn immediately when hostilities ended. Queues formed outside Employment Exchanges; as early as November 1918, *The Times* reported 2,000 women queuing in Liverpool and demanded the government release raw materials to enable manufacturers to restart business and re-employ the 'patriotic' women who had helped in the war effort. Few had by then taken up the demobilisation payments available to them, and most clearly wanted to continue in work despite the fact that their patriotic duty to support the war effort was now being replaced by a duty to give employment up in favour of men. Later reports confirmed this desire to work, not only amongst those women who had been widowed by the war, or were still waiting for their husbands to be demobilised, but also amongst young, single women. Many young women were now, due to their period of war work, over-qualified and unwilling to start again on the bottom rung in another low paid industry.

The press quickly turned against these women. Within weeks of the Armistice, the *Daily Chronicle* published a report under the banner 'Unemployed in Fur Coats', suggesting that girls and women, having spent all their earnings from work in munitions, were now more concerned with curling their hair and were rejecting well-paid jobs in domestic service. In fact, for women who had lost loved ones in the war, work was not simply a matter of rectifying an acute financial problem, compounded by inadequate war pension provision.

In *All Quiet on the Home Front*, Richard Van Emden and Steve Humphries discuss the example of Letitia, a woman who had experienced a double tragedy. Her son, Arthur, was killed in the Battle of the Somme in 1916, and her husband had succumbed to a chronic illness and died in 1917. Finding work in a coal office she wrote:

I am certain that going there saved my reason. The subject was sufficiently exacting for me to have to give it my whole attention. I had to stop pacing about. I had to meet dozens of strangers and try to help with their difficulties. For months I had lived with a weight on top of

my head and a tight string round my forehead. I used to feel sometimes
that it would be a relief when the knot snapped and I could give up.

Post-war jobs deemed suitable for women usually offered far less responsibility
and limited opportunities for advancement. Suddenly the appreciation of
employers and fellow workers – as well as their new-found self-respect –
dwindled, and watching men taking on their jobs at vastly increased wages
must have been doubly galling. Married women who nurtured a desire to
continue working or take up a career after the war often found themselves
barred, as many professions were only open to single women. These included
teaching, nursing, the civil service, as well as informal bans within private
companies. This was, in fact, illegal: the Sex Disqualification (Removal) Act
of 1919 was meant to prevent such discrimination. Section 1 of the act stated
its broad aim:

> A person shall not be disqualified by sex or marriage from the exercise
> of any public function, or from being appointed to or holding any civil
> or judicial office or post, or from entering or assuming or carrying on
> any civil profession or vocation, or for admission to any incorporated
> society (whether incorporated by Royal Charter or otherwise), and a
> person shall not be exempted by sex or marriage from the liability to
> serve as a juror.

Despite this provision, it was rarely invoked against employers in court,
and women were frequently restricted to less well-paid, more basic jobs,
determining that they could not continue to work competently with the
distraction of marriage and family.

One cannot impose current views on discrimination and equal rights on
the past. Yet, in the aftermath of war, when only weeks before the streets
had been filled with cheering crowds, how bitter many of these women must
have felt. Did some of this anger and resentment spill over into their home
lives, affecting relationships with the husbands, lovers, fathers and brothers
to whom they were once again expected to become subordinate?

Many women reluctantly returned to domestic service, but the war had
broken down class barriers and forced many to question the perceived order

of things. Even before the war the popularity of domestic service was waning, and the post-war shortage of servants required employers to offer better conditions to retain those tempted by more remunerative factory, shop or waitressing work – all with set hours and more time off. Susan Grayzel, in *Women and the First World War*, argues that: 'the extent to which individual women had better employment opportunities in the post-war world thus depended on nation, class, education, age and other factors; there was no clear sense that the war had benefited women overall'.

Sweeping generalisations about how the First World War created opportunities and liberated the female workforce can be countered by the fact that a woman's weekly wage in 1931 had returned to its pre-war average of half the male rate in many industries. Professions may have been opened up to women, and successful individuals made the headlines. However, analysis of women's share of top jobs in the 60 years between 1911 and 1971 shows how little real progress was made. Apart from doctors, the percentages of women in professions such as accountancy and the law remained in single figures.

By the end of the Great War, women could be justified in thinking themselves surplus to the requirements of a male dominated society. The marriage market and the job market were equally out of reach to many women, who may have been desperate for either option, or simply seeking something to distract them from the despair of loss.

Women and 'New' Psychiatry

The work undertaken by William Rivers and Lewis Yealland with soldiers suffering from shell shock or 'war neurosis' would influence the ways in which women's mental health treatment was administered over the next four decades. Technological advances and the development of psychoanalysis would also profoundly alter the concepts of gender and female sexuality as they were perceived by doctors treating mental illness.

Much has been written about the Victorian asylum and how doctors would label a woman's response to traumatic experiences, to childbirth or domestic cruelty, as hysterical. An examination of the ledgers of county lunatic asylums reveals that the reasons provided by doctors for admission to women's wards were many and varied but often included such classifications as 'disappointed in love' 'suicidal propensities' and 'melancholia'.

In *The Female Malady* Elaine Showalter looks at how cultural ideas about what constitutes 'respectable' female behaviour have influenced the development of therapies to treat mental illness in women. Showalter argues persuasively that many cases of mental illness in the nineteenth century were a form of protest by women against exploitation by men and the restrictions society imposed upon them in terms of behaviour, ambition and independent thought.

As mentioned earlier, before the Great War the term 'hysteria' was almost exclusively applied to women, although in France they had long recognised the 'male hysteric' and were consequently less surprised by the incidence of war neurosis amongst troops. Darwinian theory had appeared to supply scientific reasoning behind a female domestic role, and it followed that women would experience issues with their mental health if they tried to step outside their natural maternal roles.

Psychiatrist Henry Maudsley contended that the intellectual exertion required to educate women would cause physiological damage: 'The energy of a human body being a definite and not inexhaustible quantity, can it bear, without injury, an excessive mental drain as well as the natural physical drain which is so great at that time?…What Nature spends in one direction, she must economise in another direction.' His predictions were grim: competition, though healthy in boys, would upset the more delicate nerves of girls who could then become 'deranged'; excessive mental effort would cause problems with the menstrual cycle, weakness, headache and insomnia. Permanent damage could be done, leading to epilepsy or mental breakdown. Warming to his theme, Maudsley paints a picture of women ultimately causing the extinction of the human race if they continue to overuse their mental faculties at the expense of their reproductive capacity. Virginia Woolf, aged just 15, was told to leave her lessons and instead undertake four hours of gardening daily, to avoid overtaxing her brain.

Before the war, women were making slow inroads into the male dominated professions. The first women solicitors qualified in 1922, as did the first female surveyors, and a feminist critique of psychiatry was beginning. Female writers such as Rosina Bulwer Lytton and Louisa Lowe highlighted the difficulties women faced when attempting to countermand ruthless husbands. Lowe campaigned for more female inspectors in asylums, but at the turn of the century there were just eight working across state, private and charitable hospitals.

The 'rest cure' was a popular treatment for women before the Great War, as it became for some of the officers first sent home with shell shock. For women, however, it became yet another way to return them to a passive existence. In 1904, doctors prescribed a rest cure to Virginia Woolf, following the death of her father. Doomed to spend months in the country with her aunt, she wrote; 'I have never spent such a wretched 8 months in my life and yet that tyrannical and I think, short-sighted Savage wants yet another two…Really a doctor is worse than a husband.'

In 1912, in perhaps the most public exhibition of the repression of women protesting against male dominance, militant suffragettes on hunger strike were diagnosed as hysterical and force-fed. The language of madness was regularly used in relation to the suffragettes' cause; letters to *The Times* suggested such sentiments as 'women's suffrage will never become an accomplished fact unless the electors of this country become as criminally lunatic as the malignants themselves, which is scarcely likely'.

Working with shell shocked troops, William Rivers and Lewis Yealland pioneered treatments that would influence those also used on women, but truly enlightened progress was not to be made for decades. Despite the further influence of Sigmund Freud and the development of talking therapies, women were to be subjected to many years of male-dominated psychotherapeutic thought and experimental treatment. It was not until 1927, and only after much discussion, that women doctors were employed in London County Council mental hospitals.

The number of women diagnosed as hysterical did fall during the war. For some, the war had provided the opportunity to undertake meaningful work for the first time. This was especially significant for those middle class women apparently more vulnerable to nervous complaints. A real crisis brought out the best in women it seemed, so it is remarkable that little thought was given to what they would be allowed to achieve after the war ended.

Chapter Five

Suffer the Little Children:
Protecting the Next Generations

Many assume that children caught up in traumatic situations recover more quickly than adults. They are described as 'resilient'; they 'bounce back'. Perhaps, in some situations and in the short term, this is so, but when tragedy strikes, mental health professionals in the twenty-first century recognise that support should be available to help children and young people make sense of seemingly random episodes of killing and destruction.

In Britain during the First World War hundreds of thousands of children would have experienced bereavement, the loss of a home or the return of a father much changed. Hundreds would have seen first-hand the aftermath of the first air raids on towns and cities and witnessed the aircraft of a foreign power in the skies above their homes. These children were acutely vulnerable, but as the support they might have needed from mental health professionals was not available, how did they cope? What were the repercussions for them, and for their families, in later years?

Photographs and stories of the Great War, especially those revealed by veterans of the conflict and their children, often depict the very young man as the typical soldier. However, in the first years of the war, many soldiers were professionally trained reservists, older men with grown families who could understand their absence from home. If the worst should happen, the loss would be acute, but it was accepted as a risk of the job. As men rushed to volunteer, making provision for their families' emotional and financial well-being should they be killed may not have been given sufficient thought. In working class families the death of a parent threatened the loss of income and long-term financial insecurity; an elder child might suddenly find themselves the main breadwinner, their education cut short.

Even children too young to remember their father's face could experience long-term issues as the family structure was reconfigured; a mother working longer and harder, a grandparent stepping in to support them or in later years, a step-parent to accommodate. The loss of a father figure at an early age leaves the loss, not just of the person one knew, but the relationship which might have been. Mabel Hunter, quoted in *The Quick and the Dead* by Richard Van Emden, described how she coped with her mother's remarriage, whilst retaining her own memories of her father:

> I knew then that Dad was not coming back and that Tom Fawcett was standing in for him and I had to make the best of life because Mum was happy enough and my brother accepted him as his dad. As far as I was concerned Tom wasn't my dad, he was my mother's husband, and Dad was, and still is, in my heart. I missed him but I accepted that all I had of my dad was the picture in the postcard.

Some later described continuing distress at the knowledge that after the telegram arrived confirming the death of a parent or brother, they went to school and boasted of it to friends, presumably enjoying the extra attention. Yet, if a child was supported through the grieving process and given the opportunity to talk about the lost parent, then they were much more likely to recover.

The different reactions to bereavement are easier to distinguish than the consequences of other forms of distress children experienced as a result of the war. In London and the South East of England, along the East Coast and in parts of the Midlands, children were exposed to air raids, first by Zeppelin air ships and then by the mighty Gotha aeroplanes from 1916 to 1918. This book will examine the psychological impact of these raids in more detail in a later chapter, but for children the idea that explosives could drop from the sky was as new to them as an alien invasion would be to the twenty-first century observer.

In the crowded East End of London, around the docks which the Germans were keen to destroy for strategic reasons, children were used to playing in the streets, sent out from under their parents' feet in crowded homes. The first air raids were shocking and required families to find ways to protect themselves at the shortest notice. The air raids and their aftermath invoked fear and anxiety in the population, which continued well after the war had ended.

Many children grew up in wartime without obvious emotional harm; they played on bomb sites, enjoyed the thrill of watching the emergency services at work and the flight to escape into the tube stations or under the stairs was often thrilling. It cannot be assumed that all children were seriously traumatised by their war experiences. As with the shell shocked soldier some survived, while others broke down and much would depend on the strength of the family structure and the sort of life they experienced post-war. If poverty was inevitable, their father damaged and perhaps resorting to alcohol to numb physical or emotional pain or prone to violence; then the prognosis was not good. For children in these families, the impact may not have manifested itself for many years, perhaps not until they had children of their own.

At a meeting of the Royal Society of Arts on 24 April 1918, Major Sir Robert Armstrong Jones, MD, RAMC, presented a paper entitled 'The Mental Effects of the War and their Lessons in Regard to Medical and Social Reconstruction'. He spoke at length of the ways in which, 'consequent upon the war', the sacredness and importance of every child's life had been realised. He expressed his concern that those whose fathers had been killed, or who had been orphaned by the war may face 'lower mental vigour', be less 'bodily efficient' and endure 'hunger, destitution and disease' unless society could find a way to guard against it. His focus is largely analytical and practical, offering an interesting picture of the life of the early twentieth century child, who is presented as the new generation upon whom the nation has to depend for regeneration and renewal.

In those first years of the new century, child mortality remained high, one in four babies, Armstrong Jones declared, died in its first year. To a modern audience, used to intensive therapy for premature babies, it is still 'an incredible revelation' that of 1,000 babies born in 1918, 11 died within an hour, 22 within the first 24 hours, and 36 within a month. With so many fit young men lost in a war that was still raging as he made his speech, combined with the fact that the birth rate had been in decline since 1876, the nation faced a crisis. Never before had it been as important to nurture and protect the country's young.

Armstrong Jones also highlighted an apparent increase in juvenile crime, which he argued could be met with the creation of 'amusements so as to provide them with diversions from the streets and to promote the welfare of boys and girls by offering them useful counter-attractions to loafing and the temptation to be idle'. Major Armstrong was predicting the ways in which society might develop, should no steps be taken to protect children and young adults from the after-effects of war. Well-meaning as it was, his response would be seen as simplistic by the psychoanalytical community which was developing rapidly even as the war continued.

Psychiatrist and psychotherapist Dr Peter Heinl is at the forefront of work on war trauma in the twenty-first century, and his book, *Splintered Innocence*, focuses on the effects of the Second World War. He writes from his own clinical experience, of the long-term psychological impact of early traumatic experiences of war, and the consequent impact on any children that these individuals go on to have. He has used family trees or 'geneograms' to sketch a family history over three or more generations, highlighting the scale of losses or suffering experienced by family members in the First and Second World Wars across the branches. Many using this technique have been shocked to see how trauma has appeared to resonate down and across generations. It explains why, in such programmes as *Who Do You Think You Are?*, the discovery of a Great War record belonging to a grandparent or great-grandparent can still elicit such powerful emotions.

Peter Heinl has commented: 'Unless proof has been provided to the contrary, I regard anyone who has survived the war as having been traumatised in some way or other.' A parent wants to shield a child at all costs but it is not always possible. In *The Quick and the Dead*, historian Richard Van Emden illustrates, using interviews with elderly survivors of the war, how it may not be the loss of the father or brother that most deeply affects a younger child, rather, the effect of that loss on their mother. Ellen Elston, who was just nine when she lost a father she could barely remember, commented: 'You are upset for your mother really. You are upset because your mother is upset. I could hear her wandering around the house crying, although she tried to put a brave face on it in front of the children. Yes I can remember crying and crying – for my mother – not because my father was killed.'

After the Armistice, professionals in the field had also turned their attention to the new generation and the mothers who would produce them. Sigmund Freud's theoretical post-war child was, he assumed, endlessly curious about sex; constantly seeking the truth about the origins of life. He or she became jealous of the parent who shared their gender and feared punishment for masturbation. This led, according to Freud, not to the idleness feared by Major Armstrong but to deep-rooted anxieties, phobias and a lifelong focus on sensual pleasures.

Melanie Klein was a child psychoanalyst who moved to Britain from Austria in 1926. She focused most of her work on the mind of the infant, the child's deepest fears and the way it defends itself against them. The role of childish fantasy was very important within her work and in her view patterns could continue into adult life. Klein's play therapy techniques are still used in the twenty-first century, although her views were opposed by Sigmund Freud's daughter Anna and British psychoanalysts were divided in their opinion. She posited the idea that a child will challenge the parent with aggressive behaviour, which if not regulated can lead to violent consequences. This view flourished during the inter-war years and resulted in many, often middle class women, having an overwhelming feeling of guilt in relation to their child's behaviour.

Klein also wrote of the need to free sex from the bounds of secrecy, reducing the feelings of shame children often inherited from their parents. This work, alongside Marie Stopes' *Married Love* and *Wise Parenting* opened discussions about post-war attitudes to sex, changes to which could be a means of 'laying the foundations for health, mental balance and the favourable development of character'. Major Armstrong may even have approved.

Klein and Freud influenced British attitudes to the analysis of children's behaviour and popularised the idea that a child's development could be affected by trauma, such as bereavement. Whether or how far this affected the treatment of children is open to question, as many professionals then still believed it was not possible to analyse children at all.

This was a world where populations had been decimated by a conflict so brutal that its impact was unimaginable when the first shots were fired. If those in authority on both sides had not been so aggressive, so willing to take up arms and too proud to accept that the stalemate produced by mechanised warfare would serve neither well, could it have been over by Christmas? Some campaigners, including the League of Nations supporters, the Peace Pledge Union and many of the Left certainly thought so, as they sought a new post-war world populated by men and women who would turn away from armed conflict.

When considering the emotional impact of the Great War on the young, we must recognise that children were viewed very differently in the early years of the last century. In the well-to-do family, where a nanny was the main source of affection or at least adult interaction, children may have been presented to their mother and father for just a few minutes before bedtime. Working class children spent hours playing outside in the street, enjoying a freedom denied to their peers from more affluent families, who struggled with a strict regime maintained for generations.

Many parents accepted that only harsh discipline would ensure a useful life in which duty and honour were paramount. To show any weakness was to fail oneself, one's parents and by extension one's country. As discussed earlier, this type of upbringing was at the root of much of the war neurosis experienced by officers and subalterns, as they faced overwhelming responsibility in the horror of the trenches. For many girls of this class, a restrictive upbringing meant that their contribution to the war effort was frequently limited to helping their mothers undertake work in the home, knitting socks or making clothes for use in the Red Cross hospitals. Or they may have suffered a lingering ennui, watching others undertake 'war work'.

Rose McCauley creates such a heroine in *Non-Combatants and Others* published in 1916. Alix is a frail art student, the daughter of a pacifist mother living in the country with her robust female cousins, from whom she elicits little sympathy:

> "Well we're not in the trenches," said Margot. "We're leading busy and useful lives, full of war activities … It's mother who's dwining; and Alix, though she's such a lazy little beggar. Alix is hopeless; she does nothing but draw and paint. She could earn something on the stage as the Special Star Turn, the Girl who isn't doing her bit. She doesn't so much as knit a body-belt or draw the window curtains against Zepps."

Yet, many who were old enough, like Vera Brittain and Enid Bagnold, and Alix's cousins Dorothy and Margot, fought hard to be allowed to join the Voluntary Aid Detachment or the Women's War Reserve, finding useful war work and a sense of purpose.

Practical post-war issues also affected children's lives in a number of ways. They may have lost a family member or multiple relatives but there was also the possibility of injury in air raids or of illness due to poor nutrition and many were victims of or bereaved by the influenza epidemic of 1918 to 1919. Housing was poor in many parts of Britain, and education was disrupted as the war took good teachers from schools and colleges.

In the years immediately after the Armistice, commentators became concerned that these continuing social problems had caused the increase in what was termed 'juvenile delinquency'. This particularly affected boys between the ages of 11 and 13, as they became vulnerable to problems resulting from the absence of older male role models. The courts, which ordered the birching of 2,415 boys in 1914 found grounds to order for more than 5,200 in 1917. The establishment response to this challenge was seen to be lacking. Secretary of the Howard Association, Cecil Leeson, stated: 'had we set out with the deliberate intention of manufacturing juvenile delinquents could we have done so in any more certain way?'

To blame this outcome on the war alone would be to ignore developments that had already begun before 1914. The school leaving age was low – a child could start work as early as age 12 – and many were encouraged to enter the workforce to help support their families, resulting in a large number of working adolescents. During the war, work in munitions factories offered a level of earnings teenagers had never before had access to, and it led to fears that the young would be increasingly involved in gambling and drinking, thus making them potentially more likely to become ensnared in petty crime.

These concerns were, in reality, an expression of adult anxiety about the impact the Great War had had on the moral standards of the population as a whole, rather than based on fact. In Nottingham the headmaster of a senior school, R. W. Wright, gave a speech at the city's Albert Hall. It was prize-giving day for the year 1926 and he chose to speak about the newest entrants admitted to the school aged 11. Born in the first two years of the Great War, these children were apparently 'below the standard' of previous years.

29th Battalion Canadian Division going into action at the Battle of Vimy Ridge, April 1917, under heavy shell fire. *Image courtesy of Paul Reed at www.greatwarphotos.com*

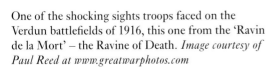

British dead from the 62nd (West Riding) Division left behind in the German trenches after one of the failed attacks at The Battle of Arras. *Image courtesy of Paul Reed at www. greatwarphotos.com*

One of the shocking sights troops faced on the Verdun battlefields of 1916, this one from the 'Ravin de la Mort' – the Ravine of Death. *Image courtesy of Paul Reed at www.greatwarphotos.com*

Electro convulsive therapy or 'Faradization' was an accepted by some doctors as a cure for shell shock, and was most notably used by Lewis Yealland at The National Hospital in Queen's Square, London. *Source: unknown.*

The more benign regime at Seale Hayne Hospital in Devon offered a distraction from the horrors of war. Here shell shock victims, wearing the distinctive 'hospital blues', make baskets in the hospital workshops. *Image courtesy of Torquay Herald Express.*

If troops had to find their own remedies for continued 'nerve' problems when they returned home, there were plenty of quack remedies on offer in the national press. Aberdeen Evening Express – Thursday 24 January 1918. © *D.C. Thomson & Co. Ltd. Image created courtesy of THE BRITISH LIBRARY BOARD. Reproduced with permission from The British newspaper Archive (www.britishnewspaperarchive.co.uk)*

STAR & GARTER HOME

TOTALLY DISABLED SOLDIERS AND SAILORS

PATRONS: H.M. THE QUEEN & H.M. QUEEN ALEXANDRA

Haven

You can never repay these utterly broken men. But you can show your gratitude by helping to build this Home, where they will be tenderly cared for during the rest of their lives.

LET EVERY WOMAN SEND WHAT SHE CAN TO-DAY to the Lady Cowdray, Hon. Treasurer, The British Women's Hospital Fund, 21 Old Bond Street, W

Special Reproductions of the Cartoon, 2|6 and f), can be obtained at above address, or, Postage and Packing free, 2|10 and fl?

It was not true that those at home were ignorant of the terrible toll taken on the troops at the Front. Pleas in the press for aid could be hard hitting. *Library of Congress.*

Having seen such images it was not surprising that those waving loved ones goodbye found it hard to 'Let no tears add to their hardship…' *Library of Congress.*

TILL THE BOYS COME HOME (1).

They were summoned from the hillside, they were called in from the glen,
And the country found them ready at the stirring call for men ;
Let no tears add to their hardship, as the soldiers pass along,
And although your heart is breaking, make it sing this cheery song

BAMFORTH COPYRIGHT.   BY KIND PERMISSION OF ASCHERBERG, HOPWOOD & CREW, LTD.

By 1914 boys from all strata of society had been taught the value of the 'heroic ideal'. From public school to the Scout movement, duty and honour were the image of what it meant to be a man. *Library of Congress.*

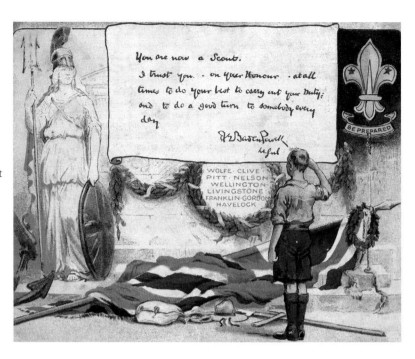

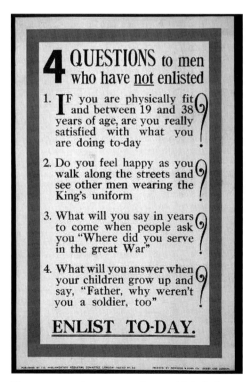

To encourage those tempted to avoid their duty, recruitment posters did not hold back in their efforts to ensure men volunteered for action. These examples mix pride, economic inducements and guilt to ensure even those least fit to serve were ready to replace those thousands already killed and wounded. *Library of Congress.*

Arthur Addison, shell-shocked, gassed and seriously wounded, suffered from nightmares all his life. *Author's own image.*

Hensley Male and his wife, Violet. The life of his family was irrevocably changed by the war trauma he experienced. *Photo courtesy of Bethany Askew.*

occa- the fish room, so that much less ice is re-
roved quired."

JEALOUS LOVER'S DEED.

Story At Inquest On Man And Girl.

How two lovers were found with their throats cut in a tenement-house in Hornsey Rise, London, on Saturday was related to the Highbury Coroner yesterday. The victims were Alfred James Hardiman, aged 35, and Mary Ellen Street, aged 22.

The girl's father, Mr Samuel Street, said that his daughter was a linen sorter. He understood that she was keeping company with a young man, although she was not engaged to be married to him. He received a letter from her on December 23, when she appeared to be happy.

Hardiman's widowed mother, Mrs Clara Hardiman, said that her son, a decorator, was a bachelor. He had recently complained of headaches. He also suffered from air raid shock.

He had kept company with Miss Street for three years. "He loved her," said Mrs Hardiman, "with a pure and moral love." They were not engaged. Someone had said to Miss Street that he was too old.

The family were quite happy on the eve of the tragedy, said Mrs Hardiman, but Miss Street had taken up with another man and her son did not like it. "I am sure he did not mean to do this thing," said Mrs Hardiman.

Quiet and Depressed.

Miss Bessie Hardiman, sister of the dead man, said that on Friday night her brother was very quiet and depressed, and next morning he prepared breakfast.

"My brother, Miss Street, and I were in the kitchen," said Miss Hardiman, "when suddenly I heard a thud. Turning round, I saw my brother standing over the gas stove with his hand in his mouth. He appeared to be choking. I shouted and fetched my brother George. Later we found the bodies on the floor, the man lying across the woman."

Her brother was very jealous of Miss Street, although he had not proposed to her.

Detective-Sergeant Day stated that he found under the dead man's leg a razor, the blade of which was kept open with a skewer string and a bootlace. There was no sign of any struggle.

The mortuary-keeper said he found an envelope in Hardiman's hip pocket on which was written, "Mary Street the cause of it all."

The jury's verdict was that Miss Street was murdered by Hardiman, who committed suicide whilst of unsound mind.

"FOR REMEMBRANCE"

Alfred Hardiman never saw action at the Front but instead suffered 'air-raid shock' which contributed to the tragedy at 49 Hornsey Rise. © *D.C. Thomson & Co. Ltd. Image created courtesy of THE BRITISH LIBRARY BOARD. Reproduced with permission from The British newspaper Archive (www.britishnewspaperarchive.co.uk)*

THE RAIDER

Reproduced courtesy of Picturethepast.org.uk at Derbyshire Record Office.

Like a scene from H. G. Wells, Zeppelin airships brought terror to the East and South of England as bombs were dropped and thousands killed and injured. *Author's own image.*

THE ZEPPELIN RAIDS: THE VOW OF VENGEANCE
Drawn for 'The Daily Chronicle' by Frank Brangwyn ARA

'DAILY CHRONICLE' READERS ARE COVERED AGAINST THE RISKS OF BOMBARDMENT BY ZEPPELIN OR AEROPLANE

Air raids were in themselves successful at increasing the number of volunteers. *Library of Congress.*

The monument to the children killed in the Gotha aircraft raid on Poplar, East London on 13th June 1917 stands in Poplar Recreation Ground. *Photo courtesy of Lynn Sharpe.*

Even before the war ended, the world was faced with an influenza outbreak ('Spanish influenza') that eventually killed more than the conflict itself. *Library of Congress.*

Post-war concerns about the health of the next generation led to the rise of the Eugenics movement in Britain, of which Marie Stopes was a leading supporter. *Library of Congress.*

PEACE, PERFECT PEACE (3).

Peace, perfect peace, with sorrows surging round?
On Jesus' Bosom nought but calm is found.

BAMFORTH (Copyright.)

Library of Congress

Despite attempts by the established church to support those bereaved and traumatised by loss, many turned to the Spiritualist Church for comfort. *Author's own image.*

Total Suicides 1911 -1928

Suicide rates rose sharply after the war, although the figures shown during the war do not include those serving in the armed forces at the time of death. *Source: Office for National Statistics.*

The ways people chose to end their lives were many and varied but the greater use of coal gas for cooking and the increasing number of cars saw gassing become an increasingly common method. *Source: Office for National Statistics.*

All Suicides by method 1911-1928

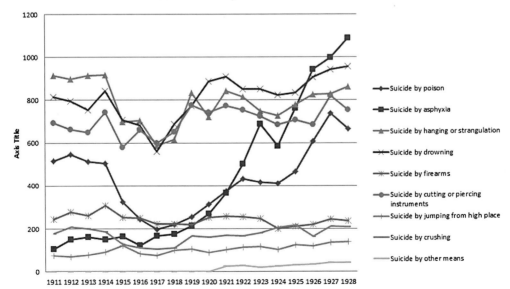

The physical and mental strain of the war had, he suggested, taken its toll. 'Stupendous in their importance' were factors connected to 'the aftermath of war – homes broken, shortage of food, half time in the schools.'

Their shortcomings weren't due to 'lazy mindedness', Wright felt, but 'physical and mental inertia' as a direct result of the war years. 'The heroism and tragedies of the fathers were visited upon the children in a very real sense', he concluded. Perhaps, Wright thought, by 1931 the post war babies would have regained their potential, yet there were no guarantees. Though the spirit of his school was 'undaunted' the effects of these mental and physical disadvantages 'prompted failure', and the repercussions, Wright believed, would be long-lasting.

A year later, Dr W. A. Potts, a psychologist and expert attached to the Birmingham Magistrates Court, addressed the Parents' National Education Conference on the subject of 'Mental Distress in Children'. Dr Potts was expressing a view that had become more widespread after the war and which was, in a sense, a response to the pre-war middle and upper class view that children should have their lives mapped out for them.

After the war it was felt imperative to promote the next generation as the hope for the nation; all those lost lives were to be replaced by new souls ready to rebuild Britain. Dr Potts warned that should adults nag and bully children to conform; demand one thing when a child might have a talent in quite a different direction, snub and deny a child the company of other children, then they could risk causing mental distress which would last a lifetime. It was accepted, Potts declared, that 'our disposition, temperament and attitude to life were largely determined by the age of seven.' Recognising the importance of the mother figure and the damage of separation, he said many 'delinquents' were cut off from maternal love. To become a properly rounded human being a child must be allowed to make an effort at a task, 'however crude the attempt', and the freedom to choose their own career. There should be no more blindly following Papa into the army.

If Dr Potts had not gone on to claim that to give a child a dummy was to push it down the slope to drunkenness, then his speech could almost have been made at any time in the last century. The earliest years of a child's life are of huge importance, confident; outgoing children are less likely to experience mental ill-health in the future; slower educational development and 'mental and physical inertia' can thereby be avoided and the children become fulfilled human beings. In 1996, the Secretary General of the United Nations published a report by Grac'a Machel, who had been tasked with looking at the impact of the armed conflict on children. Although recent conflicts have been quite different from the Great War, certain findings apply to the children of 1914–1918 as they do to those born into 21st century conflict.

Ms Machel found that children exposed to traumatic events display a wide variety of symptoms, including separation anxiety, sleep disturbances and nightmares and lack of appetite. School work suffers and older children respond to the stress by adopting more aggressive behaviour.

The report notes that following events to mark the fiftieth anniversary of the Second World War, many people recalled the sadness and pain of childhood losses and how their lives were still deeply affected by them. Although the long-term effects are hard to measure, children who suffer the loss of a parent or other close family member find that as well as the deep grief, the choices or opportunities that may have been open to them under different circumstances are replaced by a pathway that leaves them frustrated at a life of under-achievement.

Young people, on the brink of adulthood, find themselves without a role model when a parent is killed, or so severely wounded in body or mind that they are unable to offer any guidance. They often become responsible for younger siblings, who are confused when a parent becomes distracted, vulnerable and anxious.

The 1996 Report highlights how little support there was for children 20 years ago, but our understanding of potential long-term damage is better as we move into the second decade of the twenty-first century. Looking back to those years of the Great War and the aftermath, why do we expect our young grand and great grandparents to remain unaffected? What did this mean for the children born in the first 20 years of the twentieth century? Those possessing the 'resilience' often claimed for childhood would be able to put a most difficult and traumatic start to life behind them and move on. But for others the future was far less certain, 'mental distress' leading to 'ill-health' was Dr Potts' prediction of their fate.

As children were perceived as the great hope for the future, those who wanted to focus on cultivating the greatest minds and fittest bodies were developing the general view that Britain required all adult men and women to do their duty and reproduce. As this chapter highlights, however, these post-war children were part of a much wider story and one that is closely linked with the experiences of married women in the post-war years. Those who had taken up roles in munitions factories, or had stepped in to fill gaps in other professions as more men went off to war, were now encouraged to go home and increase their families.

Doctors found other ways to make middle class mothers feel guilty; it seemed that some children were experiencing sleep problems, and babies born in the years immediately after the Armistice were frequently fretful and nervous. Dr H.C. Cameron, a physician at Guy's Hospital gave a lecture in Bristol in 1921 and his 'close study' of children offered many tips for dealing with the symptoms faced by a nervous child. However, whether the audience realised it or not, his talk was actually directed more towards the mental health of the mothers of Britain's vital next generation. An anxious mother, he said, cannot calm a fretful child as her nervousness is communicated to the baby, even though no words may pass between them. Similarly, an older child unable to sleep and 'beset by introspection and fear' was often found to be an only child who had been too much in the company of adults, sharing in adult conversations carried on in his or her presence without thought to the consequences.

It is clear that Cameron was of the opinion that psychoanalysis was not useful for children and would be more effective for the mothers, 'as the mind and experience of the mother give the doctor the truest guide in the difficult problem of nervous children.' We now realise that children are quicker to pick up on the nuances of adult behaviour than was appreciated in the early years of the twentieth century. Children were not considered to need emotional support after 1918, and even if it had been available, any expression of fear or concern would have been brushed aside.

At this time children were praised for being cheerful and grown up, as if behaving like a child was somehow cowardly. During the war, newspapers had offered their young readers the opportunity to take part in the war effort. For example, the 'Uncle Dick' column in the *Southern Reporter* of

23 September 1915 set a competition to write a 'nice, friendly letter' to a 'lonely soldier or sailor' to thank them for fighting so bravely. The paper also promoted the Chancellor of the Exchequer's offer to children to take up a Post Office Savings Book (a form of war loan) to 'help Britain win the war'. 'Every shilling put into a war loan voucher is "A Silver Bullet" fired at the enemy,' it urged. Many were happy to take on this responsibility; there was no question of protecting children from the full impact of the war effort.

After the war ended and life was expected to return to normal, books and magazines published for children were unfailingly cheerful and full of adventure remote from the horrors and realities of war. *The Tamworth Herald* of 13 November 1926 highlights the latest edition of the magazine *Little Folk*, which it intended to remind parents of 'the good old days when you could hardly wait for the next instalment of your favourite school or adventure story':

> Here in the November number is the first instalment of a new school serial by Dorothy Moore, 'Tenth at Trinders' and what looks like a thrilling story for boys 'Pirate Gold' by Peter Martin … The Pets and Pastimes, the numerous Clubs, are just want children want…we can confidently recommend it to parents with the interests of their children at heart.

The target audience of *Little Folk* would have been born during or just after the war. They may have been bereaved or living with a parent still experiencing the trauma of war. In the face of such adult denial, what were children to do?

Like Ellen Elston, many repressed their emotions, trying to support their mother or other siblings; however, the distress frequently emerged at night, in dreams that their father was not in fact dead, that the army had made a mistake and he would eventually return home. These dreams sometimes continued for many years after the war had ended. As Richard Van Emden discovered, those elderly men and women he interviewed were both passive and active participants as children in the Great War. They, and others like them, had enjoyed long lives which were permanently changed by the war, often not for the better.

Hensley Male was born in 1896, in Croford, Somerset. A fruit farmer, in 1916 he married Violet and in 1917 and 1918 he served with the Somerset Light Infantry in Palestine. His granddaughter Bethany Askew, interviewed in 2014, remembers how the war had a lifelong impact on her mother, Stella Male:

> I'm not sure exactly what date my grandfather returned from the war but I do know he returned a broken man. His lungs were badly affected by mustard gas but it was his mental health that had more of an impact on the family. My mother and her older brother were brought up mostly by her grandparents. They saw very little of their father; he was withdrawn and tense and snapped at them when they did see him. He died when my mother was sixteen [in 1934], "from the effects of poisonous gas" so she had to go out to work to help support the family My mother was very bright and had hoped to do some sort of further education but instead she went into nursing, the only profession she could find where she could learn at the same time as earning money.

As the United Nations highlighted, the confident hopes of many like Stella were subsumed in the needs of family and home, and that confidence can be difficult to recapture. Peter Heinl maintains that 'the trans-generational transmission of war trauma demonstrates that the ending of wars is not dictated by historical dates.' Richard Van Emden echoes this in his contention that:

> The war hugely influenced the lives of the children of Britain for good or ill, and it continues to do so for these few thousand of our citizens who can still recall that time. And in the sense that its influence must cascade down the generations, we, too, are children of the war for, at least in part, it has made us what we are today.

Degeneration and the Next Generation

Today the term 'eugenics' is strongly associated with Nazism and the Final Solution, but it was in fact a British man, Francis Galton, who first used the term in the late nineteenth century. Galton, a cousin of Charles Darwin, took Darwin's work on the breeding of domestic animals in *Origin of Species* and considered its relevance to the improvement of the human race. He said, in his 'Address on Eugenics' in 1908: 'The question was then forced upon me. Could not the race of men be similarly improved? Could not the undesirables be got rid of and the desirables multiplied?'

The Eugenics Education Society was founded in Britain in 1907. Its members determined to campaign for the sterilisation of the weaker members of society and to prevent those it deemed 'unfit' from marrying. In 1908 Sir James Crichton-Brown gave evidence to the Royal Commission on the Care and Control of the Feeble-Minded. He was promoting compulsory sterilisation of anyone with mental illness (a term which then also encompassed learning disabilities), referring to them as 'social rubbish' to be 'swept up and garnered and utilised as far as possible.' Crichton-Brown considered that if as much attention were paid to the breeding of the human race as was focused on improving animal and vegetable stock, then the human race could be improved significantly.

August Weissman, a German evolutionary biologist, took Galton's theories to new extremes. His theory of 'germ plasm' influenced other scientists to believe in certain inherited characteristics which could not be altered by environmental factors. According to Weissman, the only way undesirable traits could be eradicated in the general population was via the laws of natural selection, however cruel the outcome might seem.

Many highly respected figures of the time actively subscribed to the ideas of eugenics. Beatrice Webb, founder of The Fabian Society was not the only left-wing supporter. Marie Stopes might be, to some, a model feminist who – with her call for a more enlightened approach to birth control – offered married women the means to avoid endless pregnancies. However, her approach to preventing unwanted births was based on a belief in eugenics and the 'deterioration of the racial body', a conviction she took to an extreme when she cut her off own son following his marriage to a woman who wore glasses. Winston Churchill wrote in a memo to the Prime Minister in 1910, 'The multiplication of the feeble-minded is a very terrible danger to the race'; economist John Maynard Keynes and playwright George Bernard Shaw were also highly influential believers in the benefits of eugenic theory.

As the bloodiest battles of the Great War were being fought, and the numbers of men returning home traumatised and mentally damaged were increasing at a significant rate, educational psychologist Cyril Burt felt able to claim that:

> However much we educate the ignorant, trained the imbecile, cured the lunatic and reformed the criminal, their offspring would inherit, not the results of education but the original ignorance; not the acquired training but the original imbecility, not the acquired sanity but the original predisposition to lunacy; not the moral reform, but the original tendency to crime.

David Lloyd George too was concerned about the ways in which the population could be affected by the huge loss of fit men to the communities of Britain. He judged it impossible for Britain to run 'an A1 empire on a C3 population', referring to the categorisation employed by the British forces as men were medically examined at the recruiting stations. This statement hints at a discussion that was to become a hot topic in the inter-war years and one which may well have prevented many people from seeking much needed treatment for mental health problems after 1918. This view implied that the war had killed off the 'best males first', leaving British society at the mercy of the offspring of 'degenerate' men.

In 1921, R. Austin Freeman, a member of the Council of the Eugenics Society, said that all 'lunatics, idiots, imbeciles, the feeble minded and "backward", epileptics, deaf-mutes, the congenitally blind, the large class of degenerates – habitual criminals, the inmates of reformatories and industrial homes, tramps, vagrants, chronic inebriates, prostitutes, the subjects of drug habits, sexual perverts and the sufferers from various congenital neuroses' should all be deemed 'unfit' to have children or, perhaps, to live at all.

This, now unthinkable, argument had a very firm scientific foothold in post Great War Britain. The pre-war Eugenics Education Society became the Eugenics Society in 1926, with high profile and influential members from scientific, political and literary spheres. Neither were religious leaders immune to the possibility of eugenics as an insurance policy against a degenerate society. William Inge, Dean of St Paul's Cathedral from 1911, wanted to restrict the population of Great Britain to just 20 million and to require each citizen to obtain a 'certificate of bodily and mental fitness'.

Although the Eugenics Society claimed to have scientific basis for their theories, the definition of who should be deemed 'unfit' was a subjective one. At the top of the list were the 'insane' and those deemed physically or mentally 'feeble minded or defective'. The Mental Deficiency Act of 1927 defined these categories more carefully, if not with linguistic nicety. They were:

1) Idiots (unable to look after themselves).
2) Imbeciles (unable to manage their affairs unaided).
3) Feeble-minded (needing care and supervision).
4) 'Moral Defectives' (deficient and vicious).

Such lists brandished by eugenicists also regularly included epileptics, consumptives, alcoholics, drug addicts, neurotics, eccentrics and the sexually promiscuous.

In 1929, the Mental Deficiency Committee was established by the government; it identified some 288,000 people or around 8.56 per 1,000 of the population as 'defective'. This figure excluded those categories many eugenicists believed to be carriers of some physical or mental disability. By the time the Committee reported in full, the figure had gone up to 10 per cent of the population or around four million people. The premise the members of the committee worked with also assumed that those with the best brains had smaller families, and vice versa.

For many influential people this classification of the population seemed vital for the health of Britain and the defence of the Empire. Before the Great War there had already been discussions about the best way to ensure those deemed incurably insane were prevented from what was commonly termed 'breeding'. Compulsory sterilisation was seriously considered as a possibility, especially as it was already legal in some US states. After the war the 'solutions' discussed included a 'lethal chamber', a method supported by some of those running British mental institutions. Mercifully, most eugenicists baulked at the idea of state mass murder to eradicate the perceived problem and returned to their preferred option; stop them breeding.

It became important for the eugenicists to ensure the public were on their side and understood the necessity for a policy of enforced sterilisation. The press were heavily involved and the issue was frequently passed off as a means of ensuring a civilised world for postwar children to grow up in. A series of public lectures was offered across all classes of society in the 1920s and 1930s, with speakers such as evolutionary biologist Julian Huxley talking in terms of 'social hygiene' and those 'better unborn'.

In 1930 the eugenicists reached the peak of their influence, as the Eugenics Society established the 'Committee for Legalising Eugenic Sterilisation' to canvas for legislation. This sterilisation was to be a voluntary procedure, except in cases where someone was 'unable to register an opinion.' Three groups were to be targeted by law – 'mental defectives, the 'recovered insane' and those suffering from serious hereditary diseases. A Draft Bill went to the House of Commons in November 1930, presented as a Private Member's Bill by Archibald Church, MP for Central Wandsworth in 1931. Mercifully the Labour Party rallied members to ensure its defeat, most obviously motivated by the class prejudice behind the legislation.

The Bill may have been lost, but the eugenicist argument was not yet defeated. After this, the Mental Defective and Brock Committee reports of 1932 and 1934 recommended 'camps' or 'colonies' of the defective, as well as sterilisation for those with confirmed inherited mental illness or 'grave disability – mental or physical'. These measures still enjoyed some support amongst local authorities, doctors and those administering full to bursting mental hospitals, but with the Labour Party focusing on the class issues involved and the inevitable opposition from the Catholic Church, any public enthusiasm or political will to pursue this English brand of fascism was lost.

Eugenicists moved towards 'positive eugenics' – that is, the promotion of healthy parents and the encouragement to those individuals with the 'right' backgrounds to have larger families. Young people were instructed to ensure that they married into 'healthy stock', selecting a mate with no history of mental instability. This did nothing much to help to those young men and women who were still finding it hard to adjust to life after the war and with a prevailing view that mental ill-health was inherited, even doctors were reluctant to father children, had they suffered from any form of neurosis.

After the First World War and the return of so many men who were mentally and physically damaged, it was felt necessary in some quarters to apportion blame. This factor appears in the discourse relating to the strengths of regular versus conscripted soldiers and also surrounding the roles of men and women in the war effort. As fertility seemed to fall after the war, just as the country needed a population boost, women were blamed for wanting to pursue a career or to continue to earn money, as they had done whilst the men were away at the Front. Some in authority even took the view that those experiencing symptoms of 'war neurosis' not related to a physical cause were cowards. E. MacPather, a witness giving evidence to the War Office Committee on Shell Shock in 1922, said: 'Cowardice I take to mean action under influence of fear, and the ordinary kind of shell-shock, to my mind, was chronic and persisting fear.'

If all therapies failed and symptoms persisted, the neurosis was frequently traced to a previous, pre-war weakness or some inherited abnormality, present before the soldier was exposed to fighting – cowards could, literally, be bred, it was believed. High profile eugenicists saw a distinct possibility that the British 'race' would inevitably be weakened if these men were allowed to father children. This may, in some cases, have been at the heart of the discrimination mentally damaged men experienced when faced by the bureaucracy of pensions and medical boards. As they came to realise, some in authority simply felt that it would be better if they did not exist.

Chapter Six

An Anxious Society:
The Many Causes of War Trauma

As Britain settled into the 1920s, fears of unrest were replaced by a general feeling of disillusionment. In 1922, the Archbishop of York gave the principal sermon to the Church Congress in Sheffield and stated that the 'spiritual heart of the present generation was restless, not simply because 'its nerves has been overstrained by the stress of war' but because 'it was suffering from a sense of disillusionment,' as both nerves and ideals had been shaken. 'Men want a true religion as never before. That is its hope. They do not find it in the church. That is its trouble.' The Archbishop was deeply concerned that at a time when many Britons felt an ongoing unease, the Church was failing them. For some this disquiet became a permanent state of anxiety, one which we may now classify as generalised anxiety disorder. But what exactly did post-war Britons fear? Perhaps the psychotherapy available at the time holds the answer.

Many people were fascinated by developments in the treatment of mental illness after the Great War. The increasing popularity of, and exposure given to, the work of Sigmund Freud offered the opportunity for some to delve into matters of the subconscious, but the shell shocked soldier was the principal subject of concern. Whether in hospital or at home, the thousands on pensions – some deemed insane and untreatable – exercised the minds of those interested in the development of psychotherapy. Dr William Rivers may have rejected the more sexual aspects of Freud's theories, which were considered racy and unpalatable at the time. Yet, his patient Siegfried Sassoon was familiar with the Freudian theories of repressed memory, and the nature of the unconscious that Rivers had used in his treatment of the soldiers at Craiglockhart Military Hospital. Sassoon, then a writer with an established reputation, wrote positively of the effect such treatment had on the officers he came into contact with. It was the equivalent of a celebrity endorsement.

Debates over which mental health treatments were the most successful in the post-war period encouraged public fascination with the subject of psychology and raised concerns in the wider population. Under the headline 'A Craze', in November 1922 the *Aberdeen Journal* highlighted a problem noted by doctors and the Church. They were worried about the number of young people, especially 'flighty young women', who appeared to 'have taken up psycho as a fashionable craze.' Having the idea that they suffered from 'repression', young people were apparently finding ways to 'cure' themselves by means of immoral behaviour, to the point that the correspondent considered the theories 'about as poisonous a plant as ever sprung up in the weeded garden of morbid curiosity and irresponsible rebellion against consecrated custom.'

In 1924, *The Guardian* reported a lecture given by a Mr Roscoe in the City of London. The speaker declared, 'It is exceedingly difficult in these days of hustle and noise for people to keep their souls alive … they lose all real grip on the essentials of life and as a result they become victims of secret discontent and despair.' As a consequence many were turning to psychoanalysis, for which he had little time, suggesting that quacks were setting themselves up as experts merely on the basis of 'brazen cheek'. Roscoe went on:

> You have a dream. You narrate it to a disciple of Freud and he tells you it reveals the sex instinct and tells you such a story that you go away wondering why you are allowed to live at all. You narrate the dream to a disciple of Jung and he tells you it reveals the instinct of self-preservance. You feel slightly comforted and tell the dream to a disciple of Adler, who says it reveals the herd instinct. All this sort of thing is more or less useless.

The public certainly had an appetite for the mysteries of psychotherapy, regularly confusing it with the more established discipline of psychology and with the psychic and spiritualist. In *The Morbid Age*, Richard Overy looks at figures from the Routledge Archive, which shows a rapidly rising market for books on the subject in the 1920s. Titles ranged from those detailing the professional techniques used by psychotherapists to others aimed at a more popular market, such as *Outwitting Our Nerves*, which was published in 1922 and in its seventh edition by the end of the Second World War. Publishers competed for the works of Sigmund Freud, who eventually signed to The Hogarth Press owned by Virginia Woolf and her husband Leonard. Although Freud was by no means an easy read, it was as true then, as now, that sex sells. His books sold to a far wider audience than the medical profession, but many readers did not understand his complex theories.

Those who could afford to approach a family general practitioner with their fears generally found the response less psychotherapeutic and more prosaic. A GP's advice to the 'nervous' patient, usually offered nothing more than a little cheer, a holiday and a tonic or herbal sedative to help them sleep. It was also commonly assumed that women had the greatest responsibility for pulling themselves together to ensure a happy family life was maintained.

In 1928 *The Nottingham Evening Post* ran a lengthy piece by a writer calling themselves 'A Masseuse', under the headline 'Nerves':

> Nine out of ten of the women I meet, professionally or socially tell me they are 'all on edge' or 'fearfully nervy' … Old ladies tell me that 'nerves' were things sternly kept under control … If women could control their nerves then, why not now? … For all our talk of the emancipation of women we have not improved in this respect. We are unable or unwilling to keep our feelings to ourselves; we indulge in psycho-analysis, introspection and auto-suggestion. And yet with all the wonderful character probing sciences, we lack the backbone our less emancipated grandmothers possessed. In a word, we are nervous wrecks.

'A Masseuse' goes on to suggest that if only a woman could keep herself busy, she would enjoy much better mental health. The idle, well-off housewife was seen as most vulnerable to 'nerves':

> Most of the patients I see for soothing massage to steady exhausted, frayed, irritable nerves are those whose greatest exercise is dancing; who rise when others have done half a day's work; who have an aspirin and

a cup of tea instead of a proper lunch, who spend the golden afternoon with their backs to a roaring fire playing bridge or poker.

This excoriating attack on the upper middle class woman further raises the issue of the burgeoning number of 'nerve clinics' established to treat these women, while the less well-off were frequently prescribed a 'rest and fresh air'. 'A Masseuse' also believed that: 'Just a little work combined with proper rest and food would cure the most hopeless of these wretched 'big bank-balanced' creatures and make a useful citizen of them.

'I am not fit for this world'

For many the pressures inherent in maintaining a settled existence both during and after the war became too much to bear.

In 1922, my great-uncle Alfred Hardiman was deeply mentally scarred by his war experience and so, when he was faced with an emotional crisis – parting with his girlfriend – he did not have the resilience to cope. As described in the introduction, Alfred committed suicide and sadly he decided to take his girlfriend with him. It is impossible to say, categorically to what extent the war affected his mental health and increased the likelihood of his committing such an act. He may have been emotionally fragile before the war started. However, the examination of newspaper archives suggests that war trauma, and specifically shell shock was regularly mentioned as the cause of similar tragedies well into the 1920s.

The *Sunday Times* of 31 August 1919 reported a 'Double Tragedy' when Arthur Nedham, a railway clerk, and his wife were found dead at their home in Leicester. With a grim similarity to Alfred Hardiman's actions, it seemed that Arthur Nedham had cut his wife's throat with a razor, which he then used on himself. The bodies 'were lying on the floor in pools of blood'; there had been a 'severe struggle' and the razor was found by Arthur Nedham's hand. It was reported that the couple had rented the rooms only one week before the tragedy. Mr Nedham had been in a poor state of health, 'suffering from neurasthenia resulting from shell-shock sustained while on active service,' and doctors had just made the necessary arrangements to have him admitted to a nursing home.

On 21 August 1921 the same paper reported the deaths of Lieutenant and Quartermaster Roderick McKenzie of the Tank Corps and his daughter Dorothy. Occupants of a ground floor flat in West Kensington, 44-year-old Lieutenant McKenzie and his pretty, well-dressed daughter appeared to live on 'the happiest terms'. In recent months Dorothy had nursed her father through a serious illness, apparently precipitated by the shell shock he had suffered with for 'a considerable time'. A resident of the block became worried when he realised he had not seen either father or daughter for two days, so called the police. As the doors to the flat were locked, the police forced their way into the bedroom, where McKenzie and Dorothy were found dead. Dorothy had been shot with a service revolver, her father shooting himself through the head with the same gun.

These are very personal tragedies. Newspapers also reported on a number of suicides directly attributed to battle trauma. Under the headline 'To save his wife', *The Sunday Times* reported on the inquest into the death of Captain Oswald Montague James KC, aged 26, of the 1st East Surrey Regiment, who had volunteered in 1914. Captain James suffered from shell shock having been wounded three times and gassed in the first attacks when there were no masks available to protect the troops. Demobbed in 1919, he had found it hard to find suitable employment and was pursuing a career as an artist. In July 1920 Captain James shot himself; at the inquest his wife produced a last letter in which he explained that he had 'committed the deed to save his wife from need'.

It wasn't only soldiers who felt they could no longer live, having experienced the horrors of war. In July 1919 *The Derby Daily Telegraph* reported on the inquest of the Reverend Arthur Cyril Hornsby Hall, the 33-year-old vicar of Turnditch who had shot himself in his study. Hall had spent many months in France, during which time he was injured, then he was later heavily involved during the fighting at the Somme. After the war he spent three months in hospital, much 'brought down' by his experiences, which he was unwilling to talk about.

On his return to civilian life, Hall had contracted Spanish Influenza and, although he recovered, he was much quieter than usual. He was then involved in a dispute in the parish over the form that the Peace celebrations should take and whether he should attend. For a vicar to commit suicide something must have gone very badly wrong. The coroner was keen to state that Hall had suffered a number of difficult experiences, which had certainly affected his 'mental equilibrium' sufficiently to make him 'temporarily insane'. Perhaps the Peace celebrations rekindled memories of the war which he realised he could never forget.

Another story published in Essex newspapers in 1919 also illustrates how the cumulative effect of traumatic wartime experiences could drive people to commit suicide, which, in the early decades of the twentieth century, was still a criminal act. 34-year-old Mary Godden was born in Leigh, Essex, but in 1919 she was living in London awaiting the return of her husband, who had not yet been demobilised. Mary contracted Spanish Influenza and went to stay with family in Leigh-on-Sea to recuperate. One day she made her way from Leigh to Southend with her young son Eric, aged two. She had decided she could no longer go on and walked into the sea, close to Southend pier, still holding Eric in her arms. A local postman spotted her and, with the help of a sailor, rescued them. However, instead of being treated with any sympathy for her plight, Mary was arrested and charged with the attempted murder of her son.

Mary Godden reportedly attributed her suicide attempt to the war and to the delay in the demobilisation of her husband, who she had feared would be affected by plans for soldiers to serve in other conflicts. She told the court:

Oh this cruel war! We were so happy, so happy. Why don't they let my husband come home? I could not leave my baby behind for anyone else. I have been ill ever since I had the 'flu. I felt so weak and everything has been a trouble. I came down to Leigh thinking I should get better, but I have got worse ...

The judge treated her kindly and the jury found Mrs Godden not guilty. Even the prosecution stated it was a 'sad case', the accused being 'of irreproachable character and a devoted wife and mother, who had tried to kill herself and her child when she did not know what she was doing.' At the end of the trial, the papers reported that 'on leaving the dock she and her husband fondly embraced, kissed and left the Court with their arms around each other.' As Mary Godden was very likely suffering from the depression that was already a recognised symptom of the Spanish Influenza, it is surprising that the case went to court.

The newspapers did not always report such cases so sympathetically. Under the headline 'Suicide of soldier who found civil work irksome,' the *Evening Telegraph* of 5 June 1919 told the story of Thomas Orchard, aged 34, who had spent four years in the army and served at Gallipoli before he nearly died of enteric fever. In June 1919 Orchard left his job as a telegraphist and walked to the railway line. Stepping in front of a train he was later found decapitated, with a note that stated simply: 'The day is one of intense loveliness; but the purpose for which I came down must be accomplished.' At his inquest the coroner did acknowledge that 'many young fellows were returning from the war with minds unhinged by what they had seen.' Despite reports that he found his job 'irksome', this was surely not enough to drive Orchard to his death.

The numbers of people committing suicide after the First World War are recorded in the mortality statistics published by the Office for National Statistics, which include useful and comparable data year on year from 1911 onwards.

Academic studies have been undertaken into trends in suicide over the twentieth century, with some key findings which are worth highlighting before we look specifically at pre-war and post-war figures.

1) Male suicide rates were consistently higher than female suicide rates throughout the twentieth century.
2) The ages at which people commit suicide differ by gender. Only during the twentieth century has suicide become more common amongst younger men.
3) Suicide methods became more or less common over the century. To kill oneself using gas became a favourite method for much of the century, as the greater use of gas cookers and wider car ownership made carbon monoxide poisoning easier. Yet the use of gas did not affect the prevalence of other methods.
4) There were reductions in both male and female suicide rates during the Great War, with the greatest increase seen in the Depression era when unemployment never fell below 10 per cent and reached its peak in the early 1930s.

The data on suicides between 1914 and 1918 does not identify former service personnel and the statistics also reflect a notable decrease in the number of people being admitted to asylums during that period. It is clear that the numbers committing suicide increased sharply after the war years, most particularly amongst the over 50s. Many of these people would have been the parents of young men lost in the war, civilians made generally more anxious after 1918, and older soldiers or officers still affected by their experiences.

The methods used by those committing suicide over the period are also interesting: immediately post-war there are spikes in the numbers who chose to drown or hang themselves; then from the 1920s onwards there is a steep rise in the number of men and women using gas to end their lives and carbolic or hydrochloric acid was also a popular, and terribly painful, choice. One might expect a post-war rise in the number of men shooting themselves, but there is no significant increase, suggesting that most firearms were handed in. Alfred Hardiman's method, using a razor to cut the throat, remained a consistently common method. In 1922, Alfred was one of nearly 800 people in England to commit suicide by 'a cutting or piercing instrument'.

A turn to crime?

Despite Lord Bramwell's concerns, there is no statistical evidence that crime rates increased significantly as a result of the First World War. The media were keen to report sensational headlines suggesting that a crime wave was imminent throughout the inter-war years, but it was not until after the Second World War that the figures really started to rise. Shell shock was used by some as a defence in court; they were stealing 'without reason', they claimed, unconsciously committing fraud or claiming they were not drink-driving but shell shocked.

There is an interesting afterword to Alfred Hardiman's actions in another case before the North London Police Court held just a few days after Alfred's death. Walter Hurrell, a 39-year-old waiter and a friend of the Hardimans, also lived in the tenement block at 49 Hornsey Rise. He was charged with 'wilfully breaking a pane of glass at the Scholefield Police Station doing damage to the amount of 7s 6d'. Pleading guilty and expressing regret, Hurrell told the story of the day he had witnessed the aftermath of the 'double tragedy' of Alfred Hardiman's suicide and murder. He had assisted the police, and had done his best to protect his children from 'any trace of the terrible affair', but later, he got very drunk, intending to calm his nerves. Instead the drink 'took him back to the trenches', and believing the police station to be a dressing station and himself wounded, he went in. Having been thrown out once, he went back in and on being ejected again he broke a window. The magistrate was very sympathetic, saying that 'under the trying circumstances' Hurrell should only pay the court costs. Evidently, such events also had a wider impact on the local community.

The widespread use of shell shock as an 'excuse' for criminal acts was mentioned in a report of the Commissioners of Prisons for the year ended 31 March 1920. Medical Officer Dr Hamblin-Smith stated:

> Doubtless in some cases this is quite genuine, but in other cases it is simply used as a catchword, and has taken the place of the 'drink' excuse of my earlier years in the service. The differentiation of the genuine cases and the estimation of the precise value of this excuse are matters of great difficulty.

It was a challenge that to this day has not been completely resolved.

'A mysterious sickness now prevalent in Spain'

In September 2001 the United States was stunned by the attack on the Twin Towers in New York, which shook the very foundations of the country. The confidence and security previously felt by the most powerful nation on the planet was seriously undermined. The population was traumatised not only by the event itself but by the atmosphere of fear and the unknown 'other' which threatened them. Would they ever be able to feel safe again?

Imagine then, that an epidemic hit the States in the winter of 2001; a disease so virulent that millions would be dead within weeks, including many who survived the horrors of New York. Eighty-three years before what is now known as 9/11, precisely that horrific scenario had occurred. As the world was moving unsteadily towards the close of the Great War, an equally devastating natural disaster was about to scythe down the survivors.

After four years of conflict people were exhausted and desperate for peace. Many had lost sons, fathers, brothers, husbands and lovers in the fighting, while others had welcomed home men who were injured, damaged both physically and mentally by the fighting at the Front. Yet, when judging how far the country was collectively traumatised by the events of 1914–18, we must also consider another worldwide tragedy, one that eventually proved more lethal than anything industrialised warfare could achieve and which heaped trauma upon trauma for many. This was an unseen, and wholly natural, enemy: influenza.

In school playgrounds across Britain, children skipped to a new nursery rhyme:

> *I had a little bird*
> *Its name was Enza*
> *I opened a window*
> *And In-flu-enza.*

The illness was at first thought benign, no worse than the common cold. Soldiers enduring the trenches in France complained of sore throats, headaches and lack of appetite. The illness was very infectious and the cramped, insanitary conditions ensured that it spread rapidly, but no one seemed to suffer the symptoms beyond three or four days and military doctors were relatively unconcerned. In fact, there had been smaller, similar and contained outbreaks of the virus in 1916 and 1917, where soldiers weakened by gas attacks had been vulnerable through contact with wild or domesticated birds. But the misnamed 'Spanish 'flu' (so called after *The Times* mistakenly reported Spain as the source) mutated and quickly became something far more dangerous worldwide. By the end of 1919, between 50 million and 100 million deaths worldwide could be attributed to the virus.

Influenza reached the shores of Britain in May 1918, striking first in Glasgow and moving rapidly south to London by June. In July 1918 London was in turmoil when 700 were reported to have died from the virus in one week. Schools all over the country closed and church attendance fell drastically as people tried to avoid infection. Over the summer the number of deaths declined, but by the autumn the disease had returned, this time causing the deaths of 17,000 in London alone. Cinemas, theatres and any public buildings where large numbers might congregate were closed down.

Then, ignorant of how the infection was spread, people were tempted to believe in conspiracy theories. *The Times* reported in June 1918 that the 'man in the street … is sometimes inclined to believe that it is really a form of pro-German influence – the "unseen hand" is popularly supposed to be carrying test-tubes of all the bacilli known to science, and as many yet unknown.' Levels of anxiety rose as the cause of what rapidly became a pandemic remained a mystery. It was even suggested in the press that the word 'pandemic' be dropped as it sounded similar to 'panic'.

Doctors were overstretched and hospital wards full, but there was no cure – the illness simply had to run its course. However, so many people still rushed out to buy up quinine and even cinnamon and snuff which were believed to be remedies, crowd control was necessary at dispensaries. The newspapers published some sensible precautionary advice; the population was advised to wear small surgical masks, ensure good hygiene and sleep in well-ventilated rooms.

Advertisements also appeared in the press from companies eager to boost sales. The makers of Bovril apologised for the shortage of the product, known for 'its immense value' at the time of epidemic, followed by a sales pitch from rivals Oxo, for a product that 'compensated for the shortage of meat', and two or three cups of which would 'provide immense service as a preventive measure'. Gas-burners were promoted as air purifiers and the company behind 'Brand's Essence' claimed that it built up 'the wasted tissues, Stimulates and Strengthens the Weakened Fibres and Muscles of the body and quickly removes that terrible "Depression" that is so likely to bring on a relapse'.

Some 'cures' caused practical problems for those resorting to them. In August 1918, Joseph Jackson, a 31–year-old soldier who had fought at Mons and returned home later with shell shock, had been recommended to drink beer for the influenza he had contracted. This resulted in a six month prison sentence for kicking a policeman when he was arrested for drunkenness.

In addition to the usual symptoms, some 20 per cent of those infected developed septicaemia or pneumonia, for which there were no modern antibiotic treatments. Some developed a lavender tinge to their skin, the sign of 'heliotrope cyanosis'. Its onset was alarmingly fast and signalled lack of oxygen and imminent death. A fit, young person could be well first thing in the morning and dead by tea-time.

Professor Roy Grist, a Glasgow physician, described the deadly impact of the infection in a letter to the *British Medical Journal* in September 1918:

> It starts with what appears to be an ordinary attack of la grippe. When brought to the hospital, [*patients*] very rapidly develop the most vicious type of pneumonia that has ever been seen. Two hours after admission, they have mahogany spots over the cheek bones, and a few hours later you can begin to see the cyanosis [*blueness due to lack of oxygen*] extending from their ears and spreading all over the face. It is only a matter of a few hours then until death comes and it is simply a struggle for air until they suffocate. It is horrible.

The lungs and major organs filled up with a thick jelly, which caused suffocation; bleeding from the ears and haemorrhaging from the mucous membranes made it a terrible death. A feeling of intense depression came over those infected and many patients who recovered were left with a lasting feeling of dejection and hopelessness.

A tragic story emerged in *The Times*, dated 6 November 1918. Leonard Sitch was a man of 'excellent character', with a wife and two children and a job as head baker at the local co-operative stores. During the war he had been subject to much abuse and hostility due to a 'foreign appearance' and to ensure his safety his employers had put out an announcement that he and his wife were born in Essex. In November 1918 the whole Sitch family had been confined to their beds by influenza and early one morning a neighbour had gone in to find Mr Sitch hanging from a beam and his wife and children dead, their heads smashed with an axe and their bodies bayoneted.

Communities large and small could be free of the infection one day and prostrate the next. Troop movements and conditions on the Front contributed to the spread, with the autumn outbreak coinciding with the Armistice Day celebrations. The circumstances required to spread infection were maximised as strangers kissed and hugged in the crowded streets.

London and other major cities were already stretched by the privations of war. After four years of fighting, British industry was severely disrupted, public services were struggling and injured soldiers were returning to their families from the very places where the virus was most prevalent. Even the undertakers complained of too much work and there were reports of a shortage of coffins. People grumbled that the trams were late, the postal service disrupted and telephone exchanges hard pressed to put calls through – all annoyances attributed to influenza. These minor setbacks were taken more seriously as they came at a time when the war had already brought many people to the brink of despair.

Tragically, the people most vulnerable to the virus were not those usually affected, that is, the old, the malnourished or the very young. This time wealth and status were no protection and the age group hardest hit were those who were actively engaged in war work: 20 to 30-year-olds. William Leefe-Robinson VC, the first man in Britain to shoot down a Zeppelin airship died of flu, whilst Kaiser Wilhelm II survived. It is still not clearly understood why this otherwise fit age group was most vulnerable. It might have been because they benefited neither from exposure and possible immunity from previous 'flu outbreaks or from the improved nutrition made available to school children through free school meals. Women were also at greater risk than men, perhaps because of rationing and having endured a cold winter, although it is hard to see why that would make them more vulnerable than young men returning from the tough conditions prevalent at the Front. Whatever the reason, it increased the pressure on already fragile minds and papers such as the *Hackney Gazette* did little to assuage fears, printing an article in January 1919 stating that 'this adds a new danger to life. One is never safe in this world.'

By early 1919 the numbers infected by the virus were gradually falling and the worst was over, although reported cases continued well into the summer of that year. Experts still dispute how many died from this strain of influenza across the world, but estimates range between 40 million to 100 million and around 230,000 of the victims were British. Other countries were hit even more cruelly; 4 per cent of India's population died, and in some parts of the United States bodies were piled high in the streets until mass graves could be dug, as nearly 675,000 people lost their lives and 25 per cent of the population contracted the virus. It was tragedy on a monumental scale.

The comparison with 9/11 is nothing more than a means of bringing home to a modern audience how deeply felt was the anxiety families endured over this new threat to their loved ones. Survivors were ravaged by weakness and damage to major organs and were often left with a lingering depression. With a health service still prioritising the repatriation and treatment of injured soldiers into 1919, many families were left to deal with infection control and lack of treatment options on their own. It is remarkable to think that the consequences of an illness with a higher total body count than the Black Death, remain a footnote to the Great War.

War From the Air – like hawks over a dovecot

Before 1914, the idea that war could be waged in the air was beyond the imagination of most British people. Authors such as H.G. Wells had foreseen the destructive possibilities of air power, but in Britain those leading the country into war were still pursuing a strategy that focused battle solely on foreign soil. Cavalry was key to their planning and, although mechanised warfare would soon be acknowledged as the key to victory, Britain was still completely unprepared for the efforts Germany had made to bring war to the Home Front.

The violation of British airspace and the realisation that both combatants and civilians were vulnerable to attack was to shake national certainties leaving an undercurrent of anxiety beyond the Armistice and into the years leading up to the Second World War. Yet, to what extent can the air raids of 1914–1918 be said to have entered the collective unconscious? Can those involved in such raids, largely the populations of the Midlands, South East and East of England and London, be described as 'shell shocked' by their experiences?

The grainy black and white images showing the Blitz of the Second World War – burning buildings, fire crews working to save buried families and the sight of St Paul's Cathedral proudly standing untouched surrounded by billowing smoke – are familiar to us. More than 60,000 civilians were killed on the Home Front between 1939 and 1945, and the casualty figures resulting from the Great War raids seem tiny in comparison – there were 4,822 injured and 1,413 killed. However, when war broke out again in 1939, the population was better prepared, and air travel for civilian and military purposes had become more commonplace.

Yet in 1914 people had no idea what to expect. From the early Zeppelin raids of 1914 to the end of the war in 1918, the British population was terrorised from the air. Germany's aim was clear as it began its air campaign. The raids had no specific military purpose, although the targets were at least nominally strategic ones – docks, railway stations and factories. The raids were chiefly used to engender panic, demoralise the population and force the government to sue for an early peace. The policy didn't achieve this aim, but it did change the course of modern warfare, as for the first time the state was unable to protect civilians away from the heart of the battle, and the boundaries between Home Front and Front Line became permanently blurred.

In the early days of the war, newspapers reporting on the Zeppelin raids of 1914 to 1916 were upbeat about the British capacity for endurance and stoicism. They accused the Germans of murder, acting as they had against the accepted rules of engagement. They praised the stoic response of the public, arguing that it illustrated how serious the German miscalculation had been. Had they expected the British civilian to respond in a different way from the soldiers on the continent and run in panic? Germans were portrayed as barbarians who had drawn the British nation together in opposition to their strategy. 'If panic is contagious,' wrote one woman to the *Pall Mall Gazette* in September 1915, 'then serenity is also contagious.'

This calm response as the first bombs began to fall on towns on the East coast of England is evident in letters from Mrs Nell Hague to her husband George, who had remained in London whilst she visited her mother in Hull. In June 1915, Hull fell victim to attacks from Zeppelin air ships and Mrs Hague was a direct witness:

"The Zeps are here! And from mother's bedroom window the whole town seems on fire … The noise is terrific and we heard the sounds caused by the dropping of the bombs … I am glad to say I never felt calmer in my life, though it is a dreadful thing to think of. Mother is in a nervous state of tension, naturally, and she thinks the whole town is on fire … One hears conflicting rumours of course, but it is apparently the desire of those in authority to suppress the details as far as possible and to prevent indiscriminate scaring."

Nell Hague's calm demeanour and thrill at being witness to the attack is further evident as she goes on to say, 'The whole thing provides a most unique experience and one which will never be forgotten by any of us… the noise itself was surely enough to wake the dead.' Nevertheless, a few days later, when she hears about the bombings in London, which she knows could involve her husband, she is less sanguine: 'I cannot tell how anxious I am about you for we keep hearing such rumours. We have been told that Kings X is blown to bits and no end of similar things. Is that so?'

Knowing that her husband may be in danger gives her a new sense of horror at the damage to Hull:

> "But oh if you could see the desolation in some parts of the town you would never forget it … The most pitiable part of all was the sight of the families coming away – they were all ordered out of the congested areas into the open – parks were thrown open and they came to the fields. It is no exaggeration to say that there were thousands of people in and around the fields and houses … the dear little children – the cripples, the aged – oh my dear it must be seen to be realised."

She understands that her previous serenity and thrill at being a witness was due to her position of relative safety and comfort. Nell Hague is now experiencing some of the anxiety, tension and discomfort previously attributed to her elderly mother. Victims of the attacks may not have panicked, but that does not mean they were not affected in some way for the rest of their lives.

Reports in the same papers offer the first clues that the British response was less than phlegmatic. At the sound of the raiders, first in airships and then in Gothas and Giant aeroplanes, many came out into the street and stared at the invaders in awe. The population had seen nothing like it. By the end of May 1916 Zeppelins were 644 feet long, with a diameter of just over 74 feet; the giant craft could hold 19 gas bags, with a total capacity of nearly two million cubic feet of hydrogen gas. They were propelled by six engines, one on the rear of a control car about 50 feet long, two in the middle on either side and three on a gondola at the rear, on the top there was a machine gun to defend the airship against attack from aircraft.

Many British civilians took away from the raids memories of excitement and of wonder, but like Nell Hague they were generally among those who enjoyed the thrill in relative safety, as one might a violent thunderstorm when sitting safely by the fire at home. Those who were directly involved in the resulting death and destruction endured more than just physical scars. Richard Van Emden interviewed many people with direct experience of the raids, who looked back on that time with clear-eyed recognition of the lasting impact it had on their lives.

In September 1916 the Germans launched an attack on the south of England, using 11 naval Zeppelins and five army airships. Many came in across East Anglia, intending to bomb London from the north. One airship dropped bombs on London Colney, just north of London, but was caught in searchlights soon afterwards. It headed northwards again, in an attempt to avoid being shot down, and dropped its remaining bombs on Enfield. The airship was flying very low and would have been a terrifying sight to those on the ground before it was eventually shot down by a British plane over Cuffley, five miles from Enfield. It created a huge stir in the press, as people rushed to the site to have their photos taken with the enemy aircraft.

But not all found the experience of enemy machines flying just feet above their homes exciting. In the *Herts Advertiser* on 9 September a description of the experience was given as follows:

> "Three o'clock approaches and the visits of Zeppelins are not at an end even yet. The plodding, churning approach of still another – the fourth – is plainly heard overhead. No 4 has evidently travelled further inland than the others … It steers a south-easterly direction after coming from almost due west, and is either making for the coast or resolving to make for London from a different angle. Its machinery throbs and rattles as it makes its nearest approach to us, and then the sound gradually diminishes as it pursues its errand elsewhere."

Many could not deal with the anxiety; the fear of the bombs was only slightly more frightening than the silence after the Zeppelins had left. When would they be back? Women in particular could be seriously affected by the stresses of wartime life. Worries for the safety of their children were unending, even if their husbands were not yet away at the front. The Zeppelin raids made these concerns more intense and many women were afraid to let their families out of their sight.

The *Enfield Gazette and Observer* reported the story of one of these terrified housewives, Marian (Minnie) Jolly on Friday, December 1, 1916. Minnie, aged 39, lived with her husband and children in Albany Road, Enfield Highway. Early in the morning of 21 November 1916, just two months after the drama of the air raids over north London and Hertfordshire, Alexander went downstairs to make his wife a cup of tea as she dressed. While he made the tea he heard a noise which, he assumed, was caused by one of the children falling out of bed. He called out to Minnie, but assumed she had returned to bed when he received no response. She had been depressed in recent weeks, more so since the Zeppelin raids, and they had called in the doctor. Thinking then that something might have fallen in the back yard, Alexander went outside and found his wife lying beneath the bedroom window, her skull fractured. The doctor was called, but Minnie was already dead. Testifying at the inquest that his patient had indeed been seriously depressed, the physician also confirmed that the post-mortem had shown a degree of disease in her lungs, which he felt could account for some of her depression and may have exacerbated her anxiety over the air raids.

Minnie Jolly's case is interesting as it reflects the links being made between mental health and physical disease just after the war ended. The medical profession noted that the number of people with tuberculosis was increasing, while at the same time mental health issues were also on the rise. *The Times*, in 1919, drew attention to this phenomenon, asking whether the two issues could be connected. The medical correspondent highlighted the pre-war prophesy by an apparently enlightened, but unidentified author, that both 'tubercle and insanity would increase after the war.' This would be due to the lowering effects of chronic illness and incipient exhaustion, which could both offer 'unhealthy soil' (quote) for the tubercle to take root in and thereby increase the risk of 'insanity' or other mental weakness, which did, the correspondent believed, remain dormant until a physical problem 'uncovered his (or her) predisposition'. The correspondent goes on:

Consequently the victim of war disease – and his number is legion – is more liable to attack than his uninfected neighbour. Tuberculosis and insanity may both assail him with a probability of success which did not exist before he fell a victim. He is, in a medical sense, a fortress the outer fortifications of which have fallen.

In relation to the Great War, shell shock and subsequent levels of TB in the population, how far did the physical disease increase the risk of mental ill health, and how far did poor mental health elevate the risk of physical illness? Certainly the Spanish Influenza outbreak resulted in significantly higher levels of depressive illness and *The Times* medical correspondent suggested that other illnesses – such as malaria, and venereal diseases – could create a similar response. *The Times* went so far as to suggest this was relevant to an ex-soldier's pension entitlement on demobilisation as, even if the physical illness manifested itself after the war, a man could ask for his war service to be taken into account in terms of the mental strain he was under.

It is now known that those with pulmonary lung disease are much more vulnerable to the physical symptoms associated with fear and anxiety, 'the fight or flight' response, which can cause a lingering depression and anxiety state. Doctors still find it hard to decide whether the shortness of breath and rapid heartbeat is caused by panic or by the disease. For Minnie Jolly this discussion was academic. It is possible that anxiety caused by the air raids made her more susceptible to lung disease, which in turn could have contributed to the deep despair that made life, even with a beloved husband and children, intolerable. No such proposition was put to the inquest, however. The verdict given was that her death was due to throwing herself from the window in a 'fit of temporary insanity'.

The descriptions offered by Edith Cadmore, whose experiences of 27 air raids were published at some length in the press in December 1919, support this theory. In the article Cadmore, a London teacher in her early thirties, wrote at some length of the excitement many people, including children, had felt as first the Zeppelin air ships and then the Gotha aircraft appeared in the skies over London. Miss Cadmore attempted to put a brave face on things for those around her, but goes on to describe the fear and physical and mental strain the raids placed on the whole population:

At first I felt only an almost pleasurable excitement about their visits and was proud that we too should be sharing some danger with our men. But one night, fear was added – fear caught from another person … Our housekeeper had gone to the nearest letter-box about 9.30 when she came running back, white and breathless, her eyes staring out of her head. "They're here" was all she could gasp, but we knew what she meant, though we did not believe her as we heard no guns. I rushed upstairs… "She's right, there it is!" There hung a Zeppelin, lit up by a searchlight, a beautiful golden pencil in the western sky. Somehow, the unexpected sight of it, the knowledge we now had of the power for harm it carried with it, added to the sight of another person's terror gave me my first real fear …

Part of the distress caused by these raids was, however, the fear that one should show fear. As time went on, I began to notice that the first alarm caused a great throb of the heart, which then beat faster all through the attack, however long that lasted; while my conscious sensation was one of sick disgust rather than of fear, and sometimes, also came the feeling that I could no longer endure the noise… What was most trying was the suspense between the warnings – when these were given – and the first sound of bombs or guns and then, when the attack was at its height the deafening noise of the defence.

As the raids continued, the media ensured that any weakness, or the helplessness men felt in the face of the enemy at home, was re-focused for the war effort. Men were sufficiently fired with enthusiasm to volunteer in greater numbers after air raids, but the feelings of frustration that they could not directly protect their families and homes lingered. When they took their place in training camps, they were seeking revenge, rather than actively protecting their loved ones. Letters home from the Front show a curious role reversal, as men wrote back of their concerns. As many saw it, they were doing all they could to beat the enemy at the Front, but the Germans, without a sense of 'fair play', were sneaking in around the back to attack their families by stealth. At least a healthy man could take some kind of action, yet the women and children were left with no option but to endure.

The general sense amongst the population that the 'Hun could not be trusted' resulted in Germans living in London becoming a target for mobs who attacked them in the street and wrecked their business premises. There were loud calls for the internment of aliens. Over 1,000 people attended a demonstration in Hyde Park in June 1916, demanding: 'That all persons of enemy origin shall be rigorously excluded from military arenas and from government employment: that all Germans naturalised and unnaturalised shall be interned forthwith including those that have been released from internment.'

British politician Sir Hugh McCalmont, addressing the demonstration, argued that it was imperative to 'eradicate the pestilential canker of Germans from our midst'. Reprisal raids on German towns were proposed but proved controversial – there was a greater need, many thought, for the services of the Royal Flying Corps to be concentrated on the Western Front. The general language of media reports and the seeming inactivity of government departments resulted in increased hatred towards Germans, which continued in the post-war years, lending a layer of meaning to the oft-used phrase 'Lest We Forget'.

The government appeared rudderless in the face of air attack. Policies raised anxiety instead of allaying fears, as in 1915 the press were forbidden to report the names of any town hit by bombing raids, thus making the potential for wild rumours greater; and the number of alleged sightings of airships went up as people became alert to every sound. This was exacerbated by the continuing refusal of the government to authorise any effective air raid warning system, for fear of inducing panic and affecting productivity in vital war work.

By 1916 the medical profession was becoming aware of war-induced nervous ailments amongst the civilian population. When the crime writer Dorothy L. Sayers suffered a patch of alopecia, her physician attributed it to nervous shock following the Zeppelin raids. There were reports that women had gone into premature labour during raids. An article published in *The Lancet* of 4 March 1916, entitled 'War Shock in the Civilian' identified a condition that was to become more acute in the next two years of the war.

Nineteen-seventeen was the year in which Britain became 'war weary'. Heavy losses of merchant shipping to U-boat attacks led to food shortages and there was government concern that an increased number of industrial disputes suggested Britain's labour force was losing faith in the war effort. The National War Aims Committee (NWAC) was established with cross-party support and grouped morale-boosting organisations and propaganda channels together to: 'keep before our nation both the causes which have led to this World War and the vital importance to human life and liberty of continuing the struggle.' This recognition that civilians on the Home Front needed support and that there must be no cracks in the British resolve, was to become even more critical. A quiet period in the air over the winter, during which the Germans had recognised that Zeppelin raids alone could not force Britain into submission, soon ended.

The morning of 13 June 1917 dawned bright and clear. A light easterly wind blew across the airfields of Gontrode and Saint Denijs-Westrem, seven kilometres south-west of Ghent, as the German aircrew of the 'England Geschwader' or England Squadron, sat down to a hearty breakfast. The day before, Lieutenant Cloessner (the squadron's meteorologist) had predicted that fine weather would continue no later than 3pm that afternoon, so breakfast was not long digested before the crews of 22 Gotha aircraft were ordered to take off. The target was London and the raid was to prove one of the most cataclysmic of the First World War.

The England Squadron had been formed just three months earlier, with a single key aim: to destroy the morale of the British people. The air raids launched from 1914 to 1916 using Zeppelin airships had aroused more wonder than panic, although more than 550 lives had been lost, 1,000 more people injured and towns and cities shaken. By the end of 1916 the German Air Force accepted that their airships could never inflict the terror attacks necessary to bend the British public to their will and force the government to sue for peace.

The development of the Gotha IV heavy bomber, with a remarkable wingspan of 78 feet, a top speed of 88 miles per hour and the ability to carry a payload of over 2,000 pounds of bombs, gave the England Squadron their ideal weapon. For the first time a plane could fly successfully at altitude over Europe to Britain, due to a built-in, albeit rudimentary, oxygen system, which supported the crew at heights where no Allied fighter plane was equipped to attack them. For the next 12 months these beasts would strike fear into the population on the ground beneath them, with their very peculiar, sonorous 'double drone' (nicknamed the 'Gotha Hum' by troops), a sound that could remain with anyone under their flight path for hours afterwards.

As the men of the England Squadron prepared for take-off on 17 June, they had several previously unsuccessful raids on the capital behind them, thwarted by heavy cloud and smoke over the City, but they knew the power of their craft. On the evening of 25 May 1917, unable to let fall their bombs on London, they had headed for a secondary objective: Folkestone. The port was key to the supply route for the British army in France, the port of departure for fresh troops to the Front, and a welcome sight to those returning wounded. But it was also a holiday resort, then filled with holidaymakers set for a fine Whitsun break. In just 10 minutes the Gothas dropped some 50 bombs on the town. Thirty-eight detonated successfully and caused more damage and casualties than anything managed by the Zeppelin airships which had preceded them.

Many residents of Folkestone gazed into the sky as the aeroplanes approached, afterwards likening the sight to a swarm of insects with the evening sun glinting on their huge wings. The crowded, poorer part of town took the full force of the raid. In Tontine Street the scene became one of unmitigated horror as clouds of dust and smoke settled to reveal the dead and injured. The owner of a wine shop left shelter to find that his customer had been decapitated. The queue outside the greengrocer's, patiently waiting for a new load of potatoes, lay strewn around a still-smoking crater. Dead and horribly mutilated people and horses were scattered around the street and blood ran in the gutter, its path occasionally blocked by body parts. Shards of glass lay deep under foot and jets of flame shot up from a ruptured gas main, while the moans of the injured mingled with the desperate cries of those searching for loved ones. Gertrude and Mabel Bawbrick, aged 12 and 9 were killed outright; their mother, who had been with them, survived, but she was scarred physically and mentally and was never able to leave hospital, dying eight years later.

Folkestone had been hit by 159 bombs which killed 16 men, 31 women and 25 children. The local and national press did not spare readers any of the grim details:

Many harrowing details of the harrowing ways in which the dead were mangled were given, it being stated that one young woman was almost cut in two; and a young schoolgirl, aged 14, had one leg taken off and the other almost severed. The five year old son of a staff sergeant of a famous Scottish regiment was reported to have had his head smashed in. Another boy, aged 11, died in hospital of a terrible wound in the left breast which penetrated through to the chest bone. It was also stated that the head of a girl, about four years of age, with light, fair hair had been found and there was no trace of the body. The child had not been identified ... The Coroner pointed out that there were two unidentified heads in the mortuary.

(*Western Daily Press*, 30 May 1917).

The vulnerability of Kent to air raids and the consequent suffering of local people was widely acknowledged as the cause of significant mental trauma. On 23 December 1917 a protest meeting was held in Sheerness 'to protest against the inefficient and inadequate warnings and protection from attacks by hostile aircraft'. One of three resolutions passed that night (alongside a demand for night warnings and bomb shelters and provision for the families of any breadwinner killed in the bombing raids) was: 'In the event of any worker's wife or family being ordered to leave the town by their medical attendants owing to nervous breakdown or shell-shock due to raids they shall receive separation allowance, the same as volunteer munition workers who have come to work in the area.'

Many areas around London were required to take in those migrating from the coastal towns and parts of London most vulnerable to attack. The general view in the coastal towns of the South East was that too little was being done to protect the population from the Gotha raids. Despite the national media's determination to portray the British public as unflappable in the face of the German bombs, locally there was less effort. The fact that a resolution was put forward, and published in the press, using terms such as 'breakdown' and 'shell shock' suggests a significant number of women and children were affected, or at least that doctors within the towns had noticed a rise in cases and wanted to make treatment available. There is little reason to suppose the population of Kent were any different from Londoners of the time, inferring more distress than acknowledged in wartime at least.

So, on 17 June, Londoners were ill-prepared and unprotected as the England Squadron came together into a diamond formation, then turned on an initial course to the north. It was a day that would shatter the lives of thousands, including soldiers like Alfred Hardiman, for a raid such as this may have triggered the chain of events leading to the murder he committed in 1922. Alfred was not alone in suffering lasting mental damage as a direct result of the bombings that summer.

A few of the original formation of planes dropped away, as technical problems – always a challenge for pilots and crew – forced them to turn back. Pushing onwards, Squadron Commander Hauptmann Ernst Brandenburg signalled the turn to the south-west; the diversionary party wheeled away to attack the vulnerable Kent coast and 17 Gothas were left to set course for London. Coming in over the burgeoning north London suburbs, Brandenburg took the formation southwards towards the City. By now, those looking into the clear skies over the capital would have experienced the first unwelcome thrill of fear and not a little curiosity. Britain's civilians were still, at this point, largely unprotected and no warnings were given of the approach of the planes, which were able to fly in almost unchallenged by British forces. People still stared up in wonder as the engine noise became audible. Many spoke of their awe at the spectacle of the planes in formation, perhaps confusing their nationality until the bombs began to fall. Observers described the planes variously as 'snowflakes' 'swanlike' or as 'little silver birds'; phrases that belied the havoc and destruction shortly to be wreaked in the streets around them.

Anti-aircraft guns were heard pumping a constant barrage of shells towards the formation, but were only able to cloud the air and momentarily distract the pilots, who dodged the hail of explosives, leaving them to fall to earth causing damage, injury and death by friendly fire. The first German bombs were unleashed over East Ham, killing four people and wounding 13, then Stratford and Stoke Newington became targets, the only warning consisted of a policeman's whistle and a cry of 'Take cover!'

Houses, schools, shops and factories were hit, as were the Royal Albert Docks. Flames engulfed buildings before rescues could be effected and the screams and cries of the dying and their loved ones mingled with the death throes of the horses caught in the blast. At the many subsequent inquests, the police gave shocking reports of finding a woman with the top of her head blown off, and another who had died of 'apoplexy' after a bomb dropped close to where she stood. A van man at a local factory told reporters that: 'The gas company's man had felt the full power of the explosion and was the worst injured of all, so far as I could see. A youth who was passing on a bicycle was absolutely destroyed, portions of his body being blown into our building as far as the back wall' (*Taunton Courier, and Western Advertiser* 11 July 1917).

Another key target that day was Liverpool Street Station, which the bombers reached at 11.40 am. In just two minutes 72 bombs were dropped, most in the streets surrounding the station itself which received a direct hit. Accounts liken the scene as the Gothas passed overhead to a 'battlefield'; buildings collapsed, a terrified population scattered in every direction to seek shelter. Horses lay dead, many falling on top of their drivers and shrapnel had decapitated and mortally wounded those who had not found safety in time. In place of shops where customers had been buying provisions just a minute before, were bodies and piles of rubble and glass.

A caretaker's wife was decapitated as she worked in the attic of a nearby house. A bus received a direct hit, with the bomb careering over the head of the traumatised driver, travelling through the floor and bursting beneath the conductor, blowing him to pieces and throwing the passengers forward, injuring and killing many. Rescuers helped the driver, who in his dazed state thought he had run someone over, but there were few other survivors. They found a girl of nine, crying; the lower sections of both her legs were missing.

As the planes disappeared, the scattered population were left to clear the wreckage and tend to the injured and dying, as ambulances and Red Cross vehicles took away the casualties. Poet Siegfried Sassoon stood on the concourse of Liverpool Street Station as the attack took place. He described the scene – an old man wheeled away, dead, on a porter's barrow, women covered in blood, and occupied train carriages flattened to the tracks. In *Memoirs of an Infantry Officer,* he wrote: 'In a trench one was acclimatized to the notion of being exterminated and there was a sense of organised retaliation. But here one was helpless; an invisible enemy sent destruction spinning down from a fine weather sky.'

Bombs continued to fall as the Gothas headed towards Bermondsey, killing three on the roof of Pink's Jam Factory. In Southwark, the British and Benington Tea Company also lost three members of staff while others were seriously injured as the basement strong room, in which many had sought shelter, collapsed, burying people in the rubble. The greatest outcry was reserved for the next atrocity, as the Gothas regrouped and headed east for the Thames, where they released their remaining bombs over the densely populated and poverty-stricken area of Poplar and the East India Dock Road. Here stood the Upper North Street School.

Of the 600 pupils on the school roll, the majority were from poor families who might have been struggling to feed and clothe their children properly, but were still ensuring that they received an education. Just before lunch, the Gothas were above the school as a 50 kilogram bomb struck the roof, killing 16 children instantly. Two died later from their injuries and 30 were seriously injured; all but two were aged five or under.

Squadron Commander Brandenburg had led his Gotha crews over the British Isles for just 90 minutes, during which they dropped four tonnes of bombs, killing 162 men, women and children and injuring 432 more. British aircraft failed to shoot down any of the Gothas, although some were lost to crash landings.

Raids continued until the summer of 1918, but German aircraft were increasingly needed to support offensives on the Western Front and any raids over British soil incurred heavy losses. However, the fear of attack remained, and many civilians suffered continuing anxiety. Reports of the lasting effects of air raid shock came in from around Britain. Minnie Jolly and Alf Hardiman were only two of many whose symptoms resembled those of the troops affected at the Front; for many, life under the constant threat of air raids became intolerable.

At the end of May 1918, Peter Pariss, aged 56, was found drowned in the River Exe by James Westcott, who worked close to the site. Pariss had apparently taken his hat off and set it down on the bank, then walked into the river at a spot close to Salmon Pool. He had fled London in October 1917, having been made anxious and depressed by the air raids, and the fear of future attacks. He had taken lodgings in Exeter, and his landlady later described him as rather prone to 'melancholy', made worse by the job he had taken as attendant on the 'mental ward' of the City workhouse. On the day of his death he admitted that he felt suicidal and needed help, but his landlady (presumably not knowing what to say and meaning to be kind) suggested he would feel better after dinner. Pariss went for a walk and never returned.

At the inquest a doctor told the coroner that Pariss had sought help for his anxieties in the ward where he worked and, after a short stay, had discharged himself, his doctor assuming a complete recovery. He had not experienced any mental health issues before the war, and no one had been able to offer the support he needed, having no understanding of the link between war trauma and mental health.

In February 1919 the *Dundee Courier* reported the death of Mr Albert Edward at the Bruce's Hotel, Carnoustie. Mr Edward, then in his mid-sixties, was the youngest of four sons of a wealthy Dundee businessman in whose investment offices he had worked. He had lived in London for many years, with his independently wealthy wife, at her home in Park Lane. Their son had fought in Egypt and returned home safely, but in the last year of the conflict Edward had narrowly missed serious injury in a Gotha raid on the City of London.

Before the Armistice, in September 1918, he, his wife and his brother became resident at Bruce's Hotel, but after six months his health had not improved. His friends had noticed his anxiety and saw a serious decline in his energy. On Saturday, 22 February 1919, Mr Edward took his brother's sporting rifle out on to the golf course and shot himself in the head. He was found by the proprietor of the hotel who mounted a search when he failed to arrive for dinner. The papers reported it as a 'tragic end…a sequel to air raid shock'.

Small paragraphs in the papers continued to speak volumes of individual tragedies around the country. In Deal, Kent, Mrs Annie Wooster had had good reason to be anxious during the war, as her son had been held prisoner by the Germans, but by April 1919, he had returned home safely. However, she had been terrified by the air raids on the Kentish coast, and in her continuing distress she went up to her bedroom, filled a bucket with water, secured her feet to the bedstead and drowned herself in a small amount of water. So determined a means of ending her life suggests a resolve to be done with the acute anxiety the war had caused her. At her inquest, the only suggested trigger for Annie Wooster's suicide was her terror during the air raids over Kent.

In July 1919, Henry Boothman went to a pond on private land in Balne, North Yorkshire. He took off some of his clothing, folded it neatly and set it down on the bank, before walking into the water to drown himself. A recent bout of influenza had weakened him and like Pariss, he had been so badly affected by the air raids that, as his wife told the inquest, the couple could no longer share a bed because of his terror and sleeplessness. Just one month later, another quiet tragedy took place as Alice Crowly, a 55-year-old housekeeper from Canonbury, committed suicide by inhaling coal gas. She had been deeply upset by the air raids and, the inquest heard, was 'haunted by the fear that they would be repeated.'

There was little that doctors could do to reassure those who were suffering from anxiety continuing long after the conflict was over. The newspaper columns were full of wonder medicines promising all sorts of miracle cures, some specifically referring to 'air raid shock', but offering little real aid. Although many people did come through the 'First Blitz' with signs of the 'Blitz Spirit' that would keep Britain fighting in the Second World War, there were still those, like one 'Mrs Brickett of 16 Binker Road, Camberwell' who swore by 'Dr Cassell's Tablets' to cure her after 'the terrible air raids' started. 'I don't know where I should have been but for Dr Cassell's tablets' she says, in an advert posted in June 1919, 'in my grave most likely.'

'I see nothing but ghosts …'

It is difficult to comprehend the scale of the losses Britain experienced in World War One. Official figures of approximately three quarters of a million men is probably a significant underestimate, ignoring as it does those who died after the war of the injuries – both physical and mental – they had sustained.

The term 'The Lost Generation' has been widely used to describe those casualties expected, had they survived the conflict, to take the country forward into the 1920s and 1930s – the 'cream' of British youth. Grief for the depleted young officer class, the middle and upper class young men who would have inherited titled estates, taken up senior positions in the Civil Service or become diplomats, for example, has been well documented. Mothers among the ruling classes took their share of the losses alongside bereaved working class women left with no income and small children to feed. Herbert Asquith (Prime Minister from 1908 to 1916) lost a son; Andrew Bonar Law (Conservative Party leader during the war and beyond) had to deal with the loss of both his sons. The poet Rudyard Kipling was deeply affected by the death of his son John (known as Jack) at the Battle of Loos in 1915. William Grenfell and his wife (Lord and Lady Desborough) lost two sons, Julian and George William (Billy) within two months and their third son was later killed in a motoring accident in the 1920s. After Billy's death his contemporary Alfred (Duff) Cooper, the politician and author, commented in a letter, 'When I think of Oxford now, I see nothing but ghosts.'

This lost generation extended much further than the officer class. Although young subalterns and officers were often first 'over the top', suffering injury and death in disproportionately high numbers, the vast majority of losses were borne by families whose hopes for their offspring may have been less ambitious but whose loss was equally devastating. The influenza epidemic took even more strong, young people.

Before 1914, the postman had been an irregular, but usually popular visitor to the homes of the working classes, yet in wartime his knock could mean the worst of news. After the war ended, those informed by the War Office that their loved ones were 'Missing in Action' experienced further anguish, as they were haunted by the possibility that a knock, or the click of the latch on the front gate could be a husband or son returning home. The surge of hope dissipated, but the state of chronic grief and anxiety, the pain of not knowing, lingered on.

For many, religious faith was the key to coping with the distress. In recent years studies have suggested that those with a religious faith or spiritual belief are less likely to experience mental health issues than those who profess not to believe in anything. Before the war, there were the first signs that the influence of the established Church was waning; attendance started to go down in what would became later in the century, a terminal decline. However, many people would still have professed a belief in God, without finding it either necessary or desirable to attend church.

One problem the Church had to overcome in the years approaching the war was its lack of engagement with the working classes. With the Church seen as a predominantly middle class institution, many of those living and working in urban areas felt themselves 'preached down to', and it took a new breed of clergyman, the Christian Socialist, to speak to them on their own terms and work to bring them back into the fellowship of the Church communion. The established Church during the war has sometimes been viewed as too ready to promote an aggressive patriotism, focusing on fighting the good fight, rather than offering the necessary emotional support to those grieving.

There was the sense that the British cause was blessed and as the war continued, any sense that clerics might be wavering in their support for the conflict, notably in the face of the call for reprisal air raids on German cities after the Gotha attacks of 1917, was met by vitriol and cries of treachery by the papers. Often a well-meaning parson would try words of comfort, only to realise that pride in the way their loved ones had lost their lives was swamped by immediate grief. They did not always find comfort in the old certainties. In *All Quiet on the Home Front*, the authors offer the example of Letitia Crow, from Hornsey in North London, who lost a son on the Somme and wrote a memoir of her wartime experiences. She described how the Church ceased to have meaning for her:

> the worst symptom was that often words conveyed no meaning whatsoever. That is really why I gave up going to church. I could hear the words, I could even give the meaning of each one and yet they conveyed nothing. I could feel, as it were, the wheels going round and round in my mind and not gripping anything. It was terrifying.

All religious denominations in Britain were affected by a decline in attendance between 1914 and 1918, and on examination the picture is even more complex. In 1914, statistics show that around 9 per cent of the population attended church to celebrate the Easter services; a higher percentage than at certain points in the previous century. Sunday School had become increasingly popular, and the importance placed upon baptism and confirmation was growing. Fewer people in the pews did not necessarily mean that fewer Britons professed a belief in God.

If the Church maintained its grip on a significant proportion of the population even in the face of its muscular position on the war, then who was it serving? As Adrian Gregory points out in *The Last Great War*, male attendance had been falling pre-war and the non-attendance of thousands fighting abroad only changed the demographic further. The apparent reduction in numbers is meaningless in the face of this absence; it suggests instead that there was in fact an increase in attendance in some churches. This increase was a direct response to the anxiety and trauma experienced by those left coping on the Home Front: women and their children.

For many the church was a central aspect of their social and leisure activities, both during and immediately after the war. Bible classes or Mothers' Union meetings may have offered a rare opportunity to leave the confines of a stress-filled home environment. This would be particularly true in a rural parish, but even in the heart of the city a generation brought up on regular attendance at Sunday School could still view the parish church as the focal point of a community. The language used in letters to loved ones in the forces and in letters to the press regularly appeals to God and to the victory of good British Christian values over the enemy.

> *God knows best – a poem*
> *I cannot say*
> *Beneath the presence of life's cares today*
> *I joy in these*
> *But I can say*
> *That I would rather walk the rugged way*
> *If him it please*
> *I cannot feel*
> *That all is well when darkening clouds conceal*
> *The shining sun*
> *But then I know*
> *God lives and loves, can say that it is so*
> *"Thy Will be Done".*

(From a letter from William Wightman of Pencaitland to *The Children's Circle*. Published in the *Southern Reporter* 18 April 1918).

From a mental health perspective, at times of trauma when the anxiety of separation, the fear of losing loved ones was overwhelming, the desire to pray for their safe return and the need to grieve and pray for the lost was natural. Children still attended Sunday school regularly, and with apparent enjoyment. This basic religious adherence meant that families could speak a common language over the tea table or by the fireside. It allowed the expression comfort, fear and grief and offered opportunities for otherwise difficult conversations, which could bind a family tightly together in the face of horror.

Of course, the opposite could still be true. In a letter held in the archives of the Imperial War Museum, Edie Bennett writes to her husband Gunner Bennet:

> It was very sad in the church on Sunday evening, the Reverend Lampen told all the congregation that he had received a special message from the Bishop that he wasn't to preach the sermon that he'd made out, but to kneel in prayer as while we were doing this our country was deciding its fate for future freedom justice and liberty … Speaking for myself I felt rotten & choked up, was all on my own as usual and had the pew to myself.

The sense of being alone with her fears is palpable in Edie's letter. Reverend Lampen was obviously not filling his congregation with hope and relieving their sense of apprehension.

The Church had appeared relatively secure at the start of the war but, as the fighting continued, it became an unofficial arm of the State and the pulpit was frequently used as a recruiting post. Sermons regularly associated the work of the army with the work of God. The Bishop of London called the nation's men to arms, 'To kill Germans, not for the sake of killing, but to save the world; to kill the good as well as the bad … lest the civilisation of the world should itself be killed.'

As fighting dragged on, seemingly without end, this bellicosity began to pall. Despite the support the church may have offered their wives, mothers and daughters, on their return ex-servicemen became increasingly frustrated with the rhetoric, which was all too frequently spouted by clerics who had no direct experience of war. Fewer could continue to shout the mantra 'God's will be done!' by the end of the war, as the belief that God could endorse such slaughter was hard to stomach.

In the 1920s, as young people were offered new forms of entertainment and venues to meet away from the watchful eyes of a local minister, there was bound to be conflict. Those in their teens and twenties, whether or not they had direct experience of war service, found the Church too eager to pass judgement on the new freedoms they sought to exploit.

The Catholic Church, with it's doctrine of purgatory already offered a 'half way house' between the land of the living and the heavenly plane. The Anglican approach to an increasing need to believe that those killed had not died in vain and would go on to a 'better place', was more problematic. There was no possibility that one could achieve redemption simply by dying in a 'just' war, and clergy at the highest level struggled to deal with the anguish of those desperate to believe that their loved ones were not lost to them forever.

A Spiritualist Resurgence

Belief in a higher plane became a great comfort to many Britons in wartime, but the reaction against established religion intensified the revival of another practice, which enjoyed something of a reincarnation during and after the war. Spiritualist mediums – who had seen their influence decline following the heights of fashion the séance enjoyed in the late nineteenth century – now became the focal point for the grief and hope of thousands.

Modern Spiritualism began in America during the nineteenth century and the tenet within it that appealed most to a post-war British public is quoted by the Spiritualists' National Union: 'Spiritualists are those who believe in a continued future existence, and that people who have passed on into the spirit-world can and do communicate with us.' Spiritualists consider their beliefs to include elements of religion, philosophy and science and to them it is a rational rather than supernatural system. Souls, they believe, survive the death of the body and enter a 'spirit-world', which can communicate with this world through especially sensitive people, 'mediums'. Retaining their earthly appearance, without any traces of the illness or physical trauma they endured in life (a relief to many whose menfolk had been victim to shellfire) they have a keen interest in the world they have left behind.

From a mental health perspective, the Spiritualist movement offered a way for women, as mediums, to receive considerable attention within a society that continued to deny them a significant role. Where some women, challenging traditional restrictions, became anorexic, depressed or labelled 'hysterical', others became prominent via mediumship. When academics dismiss the possibility of a 'collective trauma', and deny the possibility of a shell shocked nation, they ignore the popularity of the Spiritualist movement and the seriousness with which the phenomenon was treated, within even the highest ecclesiastical and political circles. Grief at the loss of a loved one is not a mental illness per se, but someone's response to it might require professional support, if only for a short period, before the natural process of recovery takes over. After the First World War there was little in the way of professional support, counselling or psychotherapy for the thousands of soldiers treated for war trauma, and less still for civilians.

In the most comprehensive discussion of the phenomenon, *Spiritualism and British Society between the Wars*, Jenny Hazelgrove offers some fascinating insights into the reasons why bereaved, but otherwise rational people, were prepared to suspend disbelief and endorse the services of those who professed to talk to the dead. Hazelgrove sees bereavement after World War One as a 'national experience' and mourning as 'a community activity', something that Spiritualism successfully tapped into.

In 1914 there were 145 societies affiliated to the Spiritualists' National Union (SNU); by 1919 the number had more than doubled. In 1937, perhaps the peak of Spiritualist popularity, 520 societies were affiliated, and huge meetings were held by the Marylebone Spiritualist Association and at the Queen's, Graham and Aeolian Halls. Individual mediums commanded audiences of more than 3,000 and demonstrations at the Royal Albert Hall were greatly over-subscribed. Numerous small circles were also established, where groups came together around a medium to hold séances on a regular basis; in 1932, according to the *Psychic News*, more than 100,000 such circles had been set up across the country.

As remains the case today, the public were fascinated with the views of celebrities and in Sir Arthur Conan Doyle, Spiritualism found one of its most effective advocates. Conan Doyle, the respected author of the Sherlock Holmes novels, as well as a physician and advocate of justice, was a confirmed rationalist. However, his family was deeply affected by several losses during wartime. His son Kingsley had been wounded on the Somme and later died of pneumonia in 1918; his brother-in-law died at Mons in 1914; and his brother, a staff officer, was killed in the last months of the war. Conan Doyle first heard about Spiritualism when his children's nanny, also a close family friend, who had lost three brothers in 1915, told him how she sought comfort by attending séances.

Conan Doyle was initially deeply sceptical about Spiritualism, but the experience of the nanny gave him cause to think again. He and his wife first attended a séance with a 'Mrs B' who claimed to speak directly with the dead, and subsequently consulted Evan Powell, a Welsh Spiritualist who communicated with the 'other side' through a Red Indian 'control'. Both apparently made contact with Conan Doyle's son Kingsley, who asked for forgiveness and reassured his parents that he was happy. Conan Doyle went on to write many books on the subject, including the two-volume *The History of Spiritualism*. He said:

> If for a moment the author may strike a personal note he would say that, while his own loss had no effect upon his views, the sight of a world which was distraught with sorrow, and which was eagerly asking for help and knowledge, did certainly affect his mind and cause him to understand these psychic studies, which he had so long pursued, were of immense practical importance and could no longer be regarded as a mere intellectual hobby or fascinating pursuit of novel research ... Evidence of the presence of the dead appeared in his own household, and the relief afforded by the posthumous messages taught him how great a solace it would be to a tortured world if it could share in the knowledge which had become clear to himself.

Conan Doyle saw the world around him as 'distraught with sorrow' and 'tortured'. He perceived that there was a communal sense of loss affecting thousands, yet their needs were not being met.

Another surprising and well-known proponent of Spiritualism was Sir Oliver Lodge, a former Professor of Physics at University College and at the forefront of research into radio waves. After his son, Raymond, was killed in 1915, Lodge took part in a number of conversations with him via the medium Gladys Leonard. Leonard convinced Lodge of her genuine talent for communing with the dead, and Lodge found comfort in the picture Raymond painted for him, through her, of a parallel world where the spirits of the dead worked, ate and lived in houses as they had done on earth.

People scoffed, but this vision of an afterlife, however illusory, was a source of great comfort to many. Even into the 1970s, famous medium Doris Stokes was talking of the 'other side' as a land of opportunity, where those who had passed over could continue with hobbies, maintain relationships and find happiness. His book, *Raymond, or Life and Death*, was published in November 1916 and was so popular that it was on its fourth reprint before the end of that year.

The influence of scientists like Oliver Lodge supported the Spiritualist movement in its endeavour to find a scientific language to describe its claims and give it gravitas. Analogies were drawn with developments in the telephone and wireless, when mediums were said to 'tune in' to their subjects. The movement also liked to stress the origins of its success amongst 'ordinary people', and to a common sense approach to the collection of supporting evidence.

The image of an afterlife was widely used as a way to comfort children who had lost a parent or sibling, or who had experienced the loss of friends in one of the bombing raids. *The Soul of the Slum Child*, by Ethelwyn Rolfe, a teacher, was published in 1929. It describes how bereaved children in the East End discussed death and the afterlife quite openly, picturing Heaven as a place where you could 'see God', 'enjoy lovely green grass' and 'see beautiful sights' – all things denied in their current lives of grim squalor. In this afterlife, their parents would see their lost children as 'little angels', and adults would be able to enjoy 'good beer'. They had created an idyll in which the dead were better off than those left behind; it was a fantasy world that no one could take away from them.

Critics called this belief in a glorious afterlife a 'menace' and suggested those who believed were 'gullible imbeciles' to fall for the 'roguery' of spiritualists. In an article published in *The Courier* in 1919, a writer expressed his concerns that so many had adopted spiritualism. 'Mothers and friends of fallen soldiers resorting to table-rapping, creakings, automatic writing through the medium of the planchette, Ouija, heliograph etc. in the hope of once more communicating with their loved ones.' Having undertaken his own research he had found mediums to be frauds, and when he confronted them with his findings, they were spiteful and aggressive. These people, he argued, were more ventriloquist than mouthpiece of the dead, and they were preying on the emotions of the vulnerable. 'There are many unfortunate beings today in our lunatic asylums driven mad by demoniacal possession. They are also directly responsible for many suicides,' he wrote. Most likely to succumb, the writer believed, were women. 'In females it often results in hysterics, chronic insomnia &c.'

By the 1930s, the Anglican Church was sufficiently concerned about the loss of communicants to the Spiritualist movement to establish a committee to investigate why so many had found solace in the practice. But after the Second World War, as more and more mediums were exposed as frauds, Spiritualism went into a decline from which it has never recovered. There are still many who believe in the possibility of communication with those on the 'other side', despite the widespread exposure of frauds. As G.K. Chesterton said, early in the twentieth century: 'No conceivable number of false mediums affects the probability of the existence of real mediums one way or the other. This is surely obvious enough. No conceivable number of forged bank-notes can disprove the existence of the Bank of England.'

To a more cynical twenty-first century population, the willingness of thousands to believe may seem incredible, but at a time of national mourning, all things seemed possible. Spiritualism, at its peak after the Great War, was truly a temporary phenomenon of an era that needed something to believe in and a community in grief. When so much had been lost, many 'could see nothing but ghosts.'

Chapter Seven

'Wild Laughter Down Mafeking Street': the Armistice and Beyond

By the time the Armistice was declared at 11am on Monday, 11 November 1918, Private Alfred Hardiman of the 31st Middlesex Regiment had been discharged from the army for a year, 'unfit for active service' due to enuresis. His service record shows that he did not see service overseas, but something had caused him to suffer from incontinence, possibly his reaction to the air raid referred to at the inquest into his suicide. Alf was now at home, with his mother, brother, sisters and nephew at 49 Hornsey Rise, struggling to find employment and cope with everyday life.

Armistice celebrations on the streets of Britain were seemingly unfettered. As the newspapers rushed to bring out special editions headlined simply 'Victory', crowds spewed out into the streets on that dull, wet, late autumn day. Although the war was not yet officially over – the Armistice being nothing more than an agreement to temporarily halt the fighting – it made no difference; the population still rejoiced at an end to hostilities after more than four years. Britain had weathered a conflict like none previously experienced, not unscathed but at least victorious. No one had yet calculated the full total of British soldiers, sailors or airmen killed, or the number of civilians killed or injured. Though very few remained untouched by loss, temporarily at least, the sheer relief of an end to the conflict raised spirits.

Central London came to a standstill, as bonfires were lit in Trafalgar Square (badly damaging the plinth to Nelson's Column) and the All Clear sounded, for what promised to be the last time. The Mall and the royal parks were packed with people keen to catch a glimpse of the King and Queen, who appeared, briefly, on the balcony of Buckingham Palace. Lorries full of ecstatic factory girls crawled through the crowds. All over the country, fireworks exploded, church bells rang out, bands played and factories, docks and ships at sea sounded their horns.

Should Germany have failed to adhere to the terms imposed by the Armistice, war could have been resumed within 36 days, but despite this the party continued. Cheering people thronged the streets of even the tiniest village; few wanted to stay in their homes on such a day. Union Jacks were strung from every available window, lamp post and shop doorway and drunkenness, even amongst young children, was commonplace. Previously respectable women were seen staggering along station platforms to catch the last trains home, some relying on their friends to bundle them into the guard's van for an uncomfortable journey back to the Home Counties. As dawn broke on 12 November 1918, many woke to peacetime with sore heads.

Surprisingly few soldiers were joining in the celebrations; some, like Alf, were still in the process of being discharged unfit, demobilisation forced upon them whether they felt their war was over or not. In *All Quiet on the Home Front*, Richard Van Emden and Steve Humphries describe the experience of Vic Cole, a young soldier who had enlisted in 1914. Vic had been wounded twice in action and hospitalised for seven months, before the shrapnel embedded in his spine left him permanently unfit for further duties. As the bells pealed and the crowds cheered, he joined in the drinking with strangers but was relieved to return home to Gypsy Hill, to 'relax his tired brain' and rest; he had been following the crowd without conviction. Many soldiers could not embrace the celebrations in the same wholehearted way civilians could. Their emotions were mixed: relief, sadness and despair at what the future might hold for them, mingled with a sense that they had achieved little on the battlefield, and anger at the loss of friends and comrades.

Florence Younghusband, the wife of General George Younghusband was on the top deck of a London bus when news of the Armistice came through. She later recalled the face of a young soldier in front of her, his face severely disfigured by shellfire. While the other passengers celebrated he 'looked straight ahead and remained stonily silent'. Despite the cheering crowds his was, in a sense, the more rational response. The crowds were overtaken by a collective hysteria. Relief and, to some extent, ignorance of the truth of the conflict fuelled a celebration that would become much more muted within just a few days, as the aftermath of war became clearer.

The truth behind the celebration is exposed in the fate of Wilfred Owen, who was killed in action just a week before the Armistice. As the church bells of victory pealed across the county of Shropshire, his parents opened the front door to see a young man holding a telegram. They were not the only family to send up a prayer that their loved ones had survived the war, only to receive news transforming their premature celebrations into a cruel sham.

Many literary figures of the day, from whom we have gained lasting impressions of the impact of the Great War, were ambivalent about the party atmosphere. Arnold Bennett, journalist and author, noticed an air of madness amongst the crowds and was glad of the foggy day to 'dampen hysteria'. Poet Siegfried Sassoon, on sick leave at the time of the Armistice, was horrified by what he saw as an 'outburst of mob patriotism' and considered it 'a loathsome ending to the loathsome tragedy of the last four years'. D.H. Lawrence told pacifist David Garnett: 'It makes me sick to see you rejoicing like a butterfly in the last rays of the sun before the winter ... hate will be damned up in men's hearts and will show itself in all sorts of ways.'

In a similar vein, Virginia Woolf, sore from a trip to the dentist, wrote in her diary; 'it poured steadily; crowds drifted up and down the pavements waving flags and jumping into omnibuses but in such a disorganised, half-hearted state that I felt more and more melancholy and hopeless of the human race.' Vera Brittain, having lost both her fiancé and brother to the conflict, could not bring herself to join in the jubilation and continued her shift as a Voluntary Aid Detachment nurse. She could only see a world changed forever with so many fit young men taken by the violence.

In many contemporary descriptions and memoirs written years after the event, the words 'hysteria', 'mad' and 'madness' are frequently used to describe the outpourings of emotion on 11 November 1918. They offer us the picture of a country that seemed to have taken leave of its senses. Looking back through the century, it is easy to feel, alongside Siegfried Sassoon, some measure of distaste for the drunken excesses, the partying and uninhibited abandon amongst the crowds of a normally restrained populace. It should perhaps be seen more as a collective sigh of relief, as though the country had taken a whiff of laughing gas to better manage the pain of four years of warfare on an industrial scale. It should not be forgotten that for the first time in centuries war had reached the shores and skies of the island and threatened civilians as well as soldiers. Certainly, the effects of the celebrations quickly wore off as the sober realisation emerged that life, as many knew it, was changed forever.

Despite the trauma many soldiers had experienced, those already discharged were perceived by some as the fortunate ones. The hostilities having ceased, many across the services believed their war service to be over, some troops on leave assumed they need not rejoin their regiments, while others thought that demobilisation would be swift and wrote home of their delight that they would soon be reunited with their loved ones. In fact, demobilisation was, in some cases, to take up to two years and became the cause of a potentially explosive situation for the government.

Demobilisation: Indecision and Inequality

Demobilisation was first considered properly in August 1917, when the government under Lloyd George created the Ministry of Reconstruction. Its head, Christopher Addison, a reform-minded Liberal, was given the task of creating a system to rebuild 'the national life on a better and more durable foundation'. The Ministry set up a number of committees to examine how demobilisation would impact on significant aspects of British life, including housing, the economy and industrial relations. This last point became crucial, as the government grew concerned that a mass demobilisation would give the much-feared Bolsheviks and those seen as determined to cause unrest amongst the British labour force the rallying points they needed. It was not an empty fear: in 1919 2.4 million workers were to go on strike in Britain – 300,000 more than in war-ravaged Germany – although there was little evidence of Bolshevik influence at the time.

Approximately 3,800,000 men remained in the army after the war ended and, although the number reduced significantly in 1919, some were still awaiting their return to civilian life well into 1920. Men remained abroad in occupied areas of Germany and in Egypt, feeling further from home than ever, and disgruntlement turned into anger, as the slow rate of demobilisation was compounded by inequalities in the way in which it was managed. In 1917 Lord Derby, while creating that first structured demobilisation plan, had disregarded seemingly obvious measures such as length of service, and proposed that each command, whether at home or abroad, should classify their men into 'industrial groups' based on their pre-war employment. This resulted in certain 'pivotal men' being returned home to work in strategically important industries, such as coal mining, ahead of any other considerations. As these men had been called up only in the last stages of the war, this meant that many men with long service records were the last to be returned to civilian life.

Subsequent small-scale mutinies at British army camps, including those in Calais, Folkestone and on the Isle of Wight could have had serious consequences. Harry Patch, who died aged 111 in 2009 and is well-known as the last surviving British soldier to have fought in the Great War, described how his company refused to parade for a peacetime officer who continued to regularly order route marches. The resulting conflict could have caused the officer to be shot. Mercifully, the anger and despair of the troops was not tested further, but as demobilisation dates approached, frustrated men began to believe that army rules no longer applied to them.

The government was further concerned by a demonstration against the slow rate of demobilisation by 3,000 soldiers in central London, which could have been a serious source of unrest. When Winston Churchill was announced as the new War Secretary in January 1919, he wisely introduced a more equitable scheme to demob the remaining troops. Churchill discarded grading on the basis of industrial necessity and looked instead at age, length of service and whether or not a man had been wounded while fighting for his country. This fast-tracked many more long-serving soldiers on the list for demobilisation and defused what could have been a disastrous situation for government, and for the men themselves, had the mutinies continued.

The Return of the Soldier

When my father and brothers, uncles, relatives and friends came home on leave and were staying at or visiting our house, I noticed a strange lack of ability to communicate with us. They couldn't tell us what it was really like. They would perhaps make a joke, but you'd feel it sounded hollow, as there was nothing to laugh about.

(Mabel Lethbridge, quoted in *Forgotten Voices of the Great War* by Max Arthur).

This world of the trenches, which had built up for so long and which seemed to be going on forever, seemed like the real world, and it was entirely a man's world. Women had no part in it, and when one went on leave one escaped out of the man's world into the women's world. But one found that however pleased one was to see one's girlfriend, one could never somehow get through, however nice they were. If the girl didn't quite say the right thing one was curiously upset. One got annoyed by the attempts of well-meaning people to sympathise, which only reflected the fact that they didn't really understand at all. So there was almost a sense of relief when one went back into the man's world which seemed the realest thing that could be imagined.

(Captain Charles Carrington, 1/5 Battalion
Royal Warwickshire Regiment).

Thousands of war widows, bereaved parents, siblings and friends were left to cope as the relief of the Armistice filtered away and the attempts to resume normal life began. Their grief was assumed and expected; harder to define and to recognise, both officially and unofficially, was the continuing unhappiness, pain and suffering experienced by those, mainly women, who had to care for men who returned from the war mentally scarred. If a man came home physically maimed, perhaps angry but similar in character to the man who went away, this created practical difficulties, but if he came home suffering from a lingering mental trauma there were greater challenges ahead.

Of those who welcomed back the man they may have married only weeks or days before he left for the Front, many were unable to deal with the transformation undergone by someone psychologically damaged by his experiences. The misery and unpredictability that affected many ex-soldiers could take a heavy toll on their relationships. Some women and children endured decades of misery, while others left, unable to reconcile themselves to a life with a man they no longer knew.

Post-war reports in the press occasionally cite inquest reports or hearsay evidence suggesting that much of an ex-soldier's continuing misery was due to the responsibility he felt towards a wife, or the heartlessness of a wife who failed to understand the extent of his wartime experience. Men committed suicide, leaving notes to say that they wanted to save their wife "the trouble" of living with them. In one such case, a newspaper reported a coroner commenting that a woman should be blamed for spurning a young man because he had returned from the war mentally fragile and hard to live with.

In reality, the support of wives and mothers saved many psychologically damaged men. In many cases, if a shell shocked man was to enjoy any kind of life outside an institution then this would be, as Peter Barham argues in *Forgotten Lunatics of the Great War*, because of a woman's patience. 'Why did some people take the route of relative independence in a domestic setting, rather than complete dependence in an asylum? The answer almost invariably is a good woman.' Some women became permanent carers; others supported a spouse through periods of crisis and some found a previously gentle man now only able to express his anger by becoming violent towards them. Domestic violence is recognised as a key symptom of *post-traumatic stress disorder* or *combat stress* amongst troops returning from conflict zones. It is still a taboo subject, even within families, and in the early twentieth century it was rarely reported and frequently accepted as the norm.

Peter Barham gives the example of Mrs P. and her husband James, an ex-soldier. Having tried to maintain her marriage for more than 18 years, Mrs P. eventually found she could no longer cope. James had returned from the Front, where he had lost his leg at Ypres. Once a relatively peaceable man, his mental health began to suffer immediately after he was wounded and his wife then had to live with frequent, often violent arguments. James P. was, at his wife's request, admitted to Mapperley Mental Hospital in 1936, where he remained for the next 30 years, before he died aged 81. A key element of this story is the response of the Ministry of Pensions to Mrs P.'s claim for a war pension after James's death. The Ministry's initial response was that she had no claim, because her husband's disability and the care he received had meant that his life was 'considerably further prolonged in this gentle atmosphere with expert supervision.'

This was a relatively common response to such claims. If a man survived for many years after the war, despite being mentally scarred to the extent that his life and the lives of his family were permanently affected, it was claimed that his eventual death, or need for committal to an asylum, was not connected to any injury he might have suffered in the war. Therefore, the widow was not entitled to financial support. Reports in the press indicate that some men left suicide notes expressing the hope that their wives would be better off financially after their death: they would have been horrified by the lengths the Pensions Committees would go to in the attempt to absolve the war of any responsibility for their deaths.

In Mrs P.'s case, she was at least fortunate in that by the time she made her claim in the 1960s medical attitudes had changed. James P.'s trauma was treated on the basis that it affected him physically and mentally, and to the extent that it suffused every aspect of his life, including his marriage. Thus it was accepted – by his doctors, at least – that however long he lived, the quality of James's whole life had been reduced by his experience at war.

Much has been written about the impact of the Great War on the relationship between men and women and the new possibilities the war had offered women in terms of freedom to work, greater independence and a move towards equality. For many women, the Armistice returned them, not quite to their pre-war position but to one with all the same restrictions they had previously been subject to, plus many additional stresses.

Admiration for those women who nursed men with serious post-war mental health problems, keeping them out of much-feared institutions despite the long-term impact on their own lives, relationships and children is not often expressed. Many saw this continuing role as one of duty, almost as a form of war work. Outwardly they would have appeared long-suffering and to be pitied, but strong and capable nonetheless. Little contemporary written evidence survives of these women's lives, but they must, intermittently at least, have seemed intolerable. Many were living in poverty, enduring poor housing and their own health problems. If their local extended family was small, or if friends had been alienated by the change in their circumstances, then it was unsurprising that, for some, the burden could become too much.

Even if a man was not physically harmed or mentally ill, the experience of life in the trenches changed many relationships irrevocably. Young men used to being constantly on edge, living in filthy conditions and always anticipating death in the next 'push', had clung on to the idea of home and their loved ones as a kind of talisman. It was natural to romanticise the domestic, hearth and home and the love of a good woman, but during home leave, reality often disappointed. Men were demobilised to wives they barely knew and children who had been babies and toddlers when they left to fight, but were now grown into thinking beings, whose memories of father took the form of a blurred black and white photograph and their mother's stories.

Many men, used to the ordered structure of macho military life, resented the control their wives had over the children and the home during their absence. Any attendant disregard for their authority exhibited by the youngsters also caused frustration. Others were saddened by the look on their children's faces, as it became clear that their father was a stranger to them. Children, like their parents were left bemused, depressed and anxious. Alternatively, deep sadness could turn to anger and suspicion, and men returned home to hear rumours of their wife's infidelity, some based on truth but others merely imagined affairs that undermined trust and left lasting damage.

Regardless of any new freedoms their contemporaries were enjoying, in the 1920s a woman married to even the most 'incurable lunatic' (a contemporary term) either had to live with the situation or give up and suffer the inevitable guilt bound up with sending her husband to an asylum. Divorce rates did go up after the war, but in most families marital separation would still have been considered deeply shocking. Women were at a disadvantage in divorce law and grounds for divorce were very limited; insanity was not legally recognised as a reason to divorce a spouse until just before World War Two. The 1937 Matrimonial Causes Act allowed women other opportunities to escape a marriage affected by war trauma when other behaviours, such as cruelty (domestic violence), habitual drunkenness or sexual offences, were also recognised.

Some historians emphasise the rise in the number of divorces after the war as evidence of the matrimonial disharmony war brought about and the greater ease with which that problem could be solved. In fact, the numbers of those legally ending their marriages were still very low. As mentioned previously, class was still a barrier for many, and for working class couples divorce was too costly. In the upper levels of society, discreet infidelity might be widely accepted, but divorce was frowned upon and women often had little money of their own. It would be many years before the majority of women could enjoy the opportunity to enter into marriage on equal terms.

For many ex-soldiers and their families, the stress of adapting to civilian life when already suffering from anxiety related to their war service was compounded by the battles involved in making a claim for a pension or compensation from the Ministry of Pensions. The Ministry itself suffered from paranoia; it was constantly alert to potentially fraudulent claimants and saw itself as the defender of the public purse against a horde of ex-servicemen and their families. Civil servants appeared to believe that the medical professionals were colluding with claimants to cheat the system, and worked on the basis that an applicant was faking symptoms of war neurosis until he could absolutely prove otherwise.

From the very first application onwards there were difficulties convincing the Treasury that applicants – even men so traumatised they had been committed to asylums – were suffering from mental illness as a result of their war experience. These men were treated as if they were as good as dead; their families were offered financial support only equivalent to that received by a widow, unlike the family of a man who was mentally fit but had lost limbs. Both men may have been in hospital, but only the man with a mental health issue had a deduction made for his care. These men could not be their own advocates, so much of the stress of dealing with authority was placed on their family.

As in cases where modern health insurance companies are quick to disallow claims by referring to small print terms and conditions, so the Ministry debarred claims from those who had experienced mental fragility requiring hospitalisation before the war. Gradually, an outcry from the public resulted in small concessions. For those committed to an asylum some years after the war it became even more difficult, as the Boards became doubly cynical that the war had played a part in the man's breakdown. Men who were able to live at home, supported by their wives, had even greater difficulty in establishing a claim.

In *Forgotten Lunatics of the Great War*, Peter Barham recounts the story of Frank Barraclough and his struggles to obtain a pension for his son James, who was convalescing at home after a period in a mental hospital suffering from the effects of his war experience. Mr Barraclough endured numerous frustrations familiar to anyone dealing with a faceless government department. He sent letters, which were passed on to multiple departments all operating quite separately from one another; he found that different offices responded in different ways, leaving his son's claim in limbo; and long-awaited meetings offered little and then resulted in more confusing correspondence.

Eventually Mr Barraclough sent a desperate plea: 'I have hitherto shunned all other sources and dealt solely, officially – must I be compelled to consult someone, or are you really prepared to act? Surely one has anxiety enough without this additional, callous delay?' Poor Mr Barraclough had tried to do everything properly and officially; one can feel his despair 100 years on.

Although much has been made of the links between the Peace settlements and treaties at the end of World War One and the causes of World War Two, there were more immediate conflicts to face for the service personnel eager to return home. Continued pressure on the armed forces came from the Anglo–Irish war between 1919 to 1921, in which troops unsuccessfully attempted to suppress the guerrilla tactics employed by the Irish Republican Army. Similarly, the repression committed in the name of Empire in India, including the Amritsar Massacre in April 1919, led to an eventual loosening of control and growing support for Indian independence. Further disturbances across British territory required significant deployment of troops, particularly in the Middle East.

In *Aftershocks*, Susan Kingsley-Kent, has argued that the public response to these crises and other unrest that took place in the years following the war, such as the numerous post war industrial disputes, provide examples of the shell shock experienced by the whole nation after World War One. Perhaps too strong an assumption, it is nevertheless suggestive of a level of unease within government and the military establishment that continued well into the 1920s. It also meant a continuing loss of life as a steady trickle of men returned home wounded in both body and mind.

In Britain, resulting changes appeared, at first, to favour the working classes who saw their wages rise and working hours reduce, as the standard of living improved for many families. Workers could at last exert pressure on unscrupulous employers by joining a Trades Union and, although unemployment remained in double figures, there was greater financial support available to those without work. Those with significant wealth were taxed at higher rates post-war, and the Labour Party made inroads to be accepted as a conceivable alternative to the Conservative and Liberal parties. This did not last; the Depression of the 1920s halted any progress the parties of the Left might have made, as state control over major industry ended. Trades Union membership went down and unemployment remained at 10 per cent, despite periods when the Labour party wielded genuine power.

As soldiers endured the final weeks of war, and subsequent demobilisation, they clung to the pre-war vision of Britain to justify their involvement in the war and give them hope for the future. The return home, resulting sometimes in utter disillusionment – if not with their family, then with working conditions, poor housing and money troubles – could reduce a man to the point of breakdown. His anger and frustration would naturally be vented on those around him, also affecting his family and community. It was common, too for men to reject old bonds and to turn back to former comrades and to the military system. After all, those men he had served alongside could now better understand him, than his wife and children.

Some men recognised, if not in the trenches then soon after their return home, that the whole experience of war would change their view of the world forever. The Industrial Revolution had wrought changes to the working lives of millions, with even the most rural of industries affected, but never before had men considered that there would be no escape from the power and destructive capabilities of the machinery of war. They appreciated this long before those on the Home Front saw the true impact of the new technologies and the scale of the change that vehicles or electronic equipment for example, would wreak on their lives, and this change only added to the sense of alienation many felt on their return.

Perhaps families could not be expected to understand the trauma of losing pals, or the bonds that developed between ranks in the trenches. Yet to find people lacking an understanding of the barrage of shells, the burning of the gas in the lungs of a soldier and the reliance on new and bigger guns to kill in greater numbers, isolated many veterans. They knew of horrors others could only imagine, they had seen as realities the images that haunted the nightmares of those back home; they had been defenceless against the war machine both human and technological. It was as if they had glimpsed a future dreamed up by H.G. Wells, and returned home to a world living in the past.

We still talk of re-integrating those with mental health problems into the community, as if they were somehow other than human; something to be remoulded and retrained in the ways of 'normal' society. Post–war soldiers could have been forgiven for thinking that, having given up their place as a solid citizen of a well-structured society, they could expect a greater effort to re-educate the world they came back to, rather than to approach the issue from the other way round. What, after all, was 'normal'?

Not all felt powerless of course; many used the guilt and fear they could provoke in the minds of the public and the authorities to ensure they achieved a position of respect, even if it was through less than admirable means. Today, the media may use the knowledge that a victim of injustice is a war veteran to elicit a heightened response, even if it is to highlight something as trivial as an inaccurate gas bill or poor service in a shop. It leaves the reader with the uncomfortable feeling of having been manipulated. But for many First World War veterans, the phrase 'look what I sacrificed for you' had real meaning. It created less fear in a community than a man threatening physical violence or joining with others to argue vehemently for reparation. Some veterans, however, were left without any means of explanation, could not exert any influence and they needed a language to express the experience of war. There were no words.

Perhaps British veterans were responding to the feeling of injustice that spread amongst some sections of the population after the Armistice. To returning soldiers it could seem that whilst they had been enduring hell to defend hearth and home, the country they returned to had been doing very nicely in their absence. Siegfried Sassoon put this feeling most eloquently in the letter that resulted in his admittance to Craiglockhart Military Hospital, ostensibly suffering from shell shock:

> On behalf of those who are suffering now I make this protest against
> the deception which is being practised on them; also I believe that I
> may help to destroy the callous complacency with which the majority

of those at home regard the contrivance of agonies which they do not, and which they have not sufficient imagination to realize.

Men like Sassoon wanted society to continue to feel collective guilt for the hellish experience that soldiers had gone through and for the widespread indifference they had received on their return. From domestic life to national campaigns, there was a sense that the nation could never understand or do enough.

Whilst the war still raged and home leave became harder to endure, many had become more closely attached to their comrades, making every loss harder to bear and increasing the psychological impact of bereavement. After the war ended, only their old comrades and some of the memorials allowed their sacrifice to remain visible. Some found this a healthy way to mourn and then to move on; others lived on with what we now refer to as survivor guilt and a bitter sense of injustice, expressed as a hatred of those who had not suffered as they had, which could last for years, if not the rest of their lives.

Men may have survived four years of war, only to return home and gradually decline into long term mental illness, including schizophrenia. W.H.R. Rivers, who treated Siegfried Sassoon at Craiglockhart Military Hospital, was of the opinion that the encouragement after demobilisation to go home and 'forget about the war' was the worst possible advice. Trying to forget would merely lodge memories deeper in a soldier's thoughts.

Charles Carrington was born in 1897 and signed up for military service aged just 17. By 1918 he was an officer of distinction, winning the Military Cross and serving on Western and Italian Fronts. Never to blame the authorities for encouraging young men into a disastrous conflict, he believed most had known exactly what they were getting into, though his memoirs, published in 1929, also highlighted the psychological problems the conflict caused veterans. Using the pseudonym 'C. Edmonds' he called the book *A Subaltern's War*. It underlined the issues faced by many in post-war Britain – the disillusionment and austerity, homecomings blighted by disappointment, and the silence these created, as men tried to repress the horrible memories they had come home with.

By 1929 Carrington, and many other veterans, had found their voice at last, and an outpouring of literary effort replaced the silence of the previous decade. He felt that the darkness of the previous 10 years had brought the population, those affected by the war and those less directly impacted, together in a sort of collective trauma. The returning soldier, silenced by his alienation, was in some way liberated when a greater part of the national population was equally despondent and oppressed by events outside their control.

Oddly, British soldiers returning after the war were denied the release that came for others with defeat. Soldiers in the central powers could vent their anger by attacking the systems that had sent them to war by initiating direct action and revolution. British politicians, particularly during the industrial unrest of 1919, were genuinely concerned that revolutionary Bolshevik sentiments would prevail and the government come under attack. The men most seriously affected by the war, were often too ill to respond with the aggression necessary for widespread and co-ordinated violence. They didn't walk out of military hospitals immediately cured of their neurosis as soon as the war was over and take arms against authority; they endured frustration at a very domestic level.

Two quotes seem to sum up the post-war experience of a number of soldiers. They are not by British writers, but they have nonetheless been chosen by historian E.J. Leed to express a widespread and international response to the aftermath of the Great War. The first is by Friedrich William Heinz, a German who wrote:

These people told us the war was over. That was a laugh. We ourselves are the war: its flame burns strongly in us. It envelops our whole being and fascinates us with the enticing urge to destroy. We obeyed … and marched onto the battlefields of the post war world just as we had gone into battle on the Western Front.

The second is by the author of *All Quiet on the Western Front*, Erich Maria Remarque:

Now if we go back we will be weary, broken, burnt out, rootless and without hope. We will not be able to find our way any more. And men will not understand us … We will be superfluous even to ourselves; we will grow older, a few will adapt themselves, some others will merely submit, and most will be bewildered.

It is beholden upon us, the twenty-first century descendants of the war generation, to look back into our family histories and, without judgement, look again at the lives our grandparents and great-grandparents lived after 1918. Silence might mean submission, violence, frustration and despair, but the alternative, a life of abandon and lack of self-control, may also be one of denial and the repression of painful memories.

For some years after the Second World War little research was done into the First; a new set of precedents had been established, seemingly consigning those of 1914–18 to history. As David Stevenson suggests in *1914–18; The History of the First World War*, the 1960s and more recently the 1990s saw a revival of interest in the conflict, including a surge of novels set in the period, among them *Birdsong* by Sebastian Faulks and Pat Barker's *Regeneration* trilogy and more recently *The Lie* by Helen Dunmore and *Wake* by Anna Hope. Numerous scholarly papers and conferences offer new perspectives. Stevenson links the revival to 'generational turnover', as the grandchildren and great-grandchildren of the men and women who served in the Great War revisit their sufferings in the same way that the children of the war did in the 1930s.

Oral history boomed as historians sought, and still seek, to take direct testimony from those children of the war and our fascination with genealogy and the social history of our families, along with the greater availability of official records online has reinvigorated the study of our near past. We have a clearer perspective on the war of 100 years ago now, as historians have worked tirelessly to provide accounts of the conflict that, as far as is possible, would be recognisable to those who participated in it. We must remember though, that those who took part in the events responded without any thought to making history and we will never have the ability to read their minds and truly understand.

Monuments and Memories

A century on from the beginning of World War One, on the Sunday closest to 11 November, the British nation joins together in an act of remembrance focused on the Cenotaph in Whitehall. It is a moving expression of respect for lives lost in that war and in conflicts since. The two minute silence, signalled by the eleven o'clock chimes of Big Ben, provides a brief moment in which to remember the sacrifices so many made in the service of their country. The sight of the reigning monarch and dignitaries from around the world laying wreathes of poppies and bowing to those the memorial commemorates; the lengthy march past of men and women with direct connections to the services; the sombre music played by the military bandsmen; it all means a great deal to those taking part and to others across the country and in Commonwealth countries, laying their own tokens at local war memorials.

Professor Jay Winter writes, in *Sites of Memory, Sites of Mourning* that 'grief is a state of mind; bereavement a condition', and that mourning helps survivors come to terms with their loss. This book has mentioned the anxiety caused by the dread of the telegram (or letter) informing of a loved one's death; hearing or reading reports of the battles at the front, seeing other young men coming home seriously wounded with no word of one's own child. Professor Winter quotes a woman who would later hear her husband was lost: 'Such distress, to know nothing, to be alone ... like a beast'. So many were bereaved that whole communities could come together to support each other in their grief, but those for whom there was no news were in limbo, deprived of that kinship until the bad news came. Siegfried Sassoon berated the British public for their seeming unwillingness to grasp the horrors of trench warfare, but it was in front of them in the stories recounted by exhausted men on leave, by those who worked as nurses and in other voluntary capacities in the war effort. How could they not know, and be terrified?

We also do well to remember that up to 50 per cent of all those killed had no grave. There was always the hope that military authorities has made a mistake and that a husband or son was alive and would knock on the door wondering what all the fuss was about. The families had not been able to spend any time with a body, or even with personal effects and psychologists have now long known that is important for parents who have lost a baby at birth, for example, to spend time with their child, acknowledge them as part of the family and see death in order to believe it. For so many in the First World War, there was no closure, however painful it would be. They were denied those very public rituals of mourning – the funeral, the wearing of black, the seclusion – that were a part of British Society until just before the war. Death for the Victorians and Edwardians was made a social affair, in that the bereaved were supported by a community on into their own new roles whilst seeing their loved ones recognised and commemorated. The war had changed this period of mourning in any event, as to be unhappy; to wear black and retire from society was by some seen to be unpatriotic. Mourning must be repressed and loss bravely borne.

Worse still was the telegram or letter that arrived baldly stating that a soldier was 'Missing, presumed dead'. Many men could attribute their shell shock to seeing comrades torn apart before their eyes, left unidentifiable by a shell blast. It was a death soldiers dreaded, but even though there was no body left to bury, evidence could be taken to offer certainty to a family. Not so when battles killed thousands on one day and bodies were buried quickly to avoid the spread of disease; or when a trench collapsed leaving bodies entombed in mud. How could a family undergo a period of mourning, of healing? How could they stand at any civil memorial, or take part in any service of remembrance? They had lost a child, husband or brother but even the knowledge of his death was denied them. Voluntary organisations such as the Red Cross worked tirelessly to make enquiries on behalf of these families, but many lived on with the vaguest of hopes that a loved one was a prisoner of war, suffering from amnesia or simply lost on the acres of battlefield that stretched across Europe. Women, not formally widowed but left to support small children might take their chance and start a new relationship, risking the return of a man who would find himself usurped.

So in June 1919, as the Treaty of Versailles was finally signed and war was officially over, the original construction of the cenotaph in Central London, and the 'Victory' parade that was to take place, prompted an ambivalent response amongst the population. The national mood was by this time unwilling to see any ceremony as a celebration. The victory was already being questioned and a melancholy, angry mood pervaded some sections of the population. The loss of life and lack of local and national action to ensure practical support to those expecting a 'home fit for heroes', were issues that fomented public bitterness.

The government pressed ahead regardless and, in doing so, adopted a tone that was less triumphalist and more respectful, laying the foundations of a permanent focus for the nation's grief. Sir Edward Lutyens, the most revered architect of the early twentieth century, was given just two weeks in which to construct a suitable memorial as a centrepiece for the parade, which thousands would march past to pay their respects. Mercifully, this was not the first time Lutyens had given thought to such a construction. Sir Alfred Mond, the Commissioner of the Board of Works with responsibility for the building of monuments, had already approached the great man and preliminary sketches had been made. With what may seem, for the time, remarkable sensitivity, all agreed that the simple, temporary structure, of wood designed to look like stone, should be non-denominational and have nothing on its design to alienate those of other faiths, or none at all.

In the end, the nation embraced wholeheartedly what also became known as the 'Peace Day Parade'. On 19 July 1919, despite the miserable wet weather that descended on the capital from mid-morning, London was in the mood not only to pay its respects but, eight months after the end of hostilities, to take to the streets in a more measured 'celebration' than had taken place the previous November. Within days of the first march past, whilst the base of the wooden structure was still covered with the wreathes laid by the public, the War Cabinet agreed that the wooden cenotaph should be made permanent, to act as a national memorial. An identical structure in Portland stone was constructed by Holland, Hannen & Cubitts and unveiled by King George V on 11 November 1920.

However, behind all this pomp and ceremony was also a lack of acknowledgement by the authorities of the long-term needs of the war-traumatised population. When one examines the wording of many war memorial inscriptions – not just the Cenotaph in Whitehall but all those established by subscription or donated in the years between the wars – the dead and wounded are referred to as 'heroes', who were 'proud' and 'glorious'. In reality, many of those men and their families had experienced hell. The stark, horrific truth meant that the end for many was far from 'heroic'.

Those who returned with shell shock could not feel like heroes, while subject to constant feelings of fear and inadequacy, and families of those blown to pieces by shell fire would find the glory and pride hard to realise. Charles Carrington, in his 1939 memoir, *Soldier From the Wars Returning*, wrote of his dissatisfaction with such memorials: 'To march to the Cenotaph was too much like attending one's own funeral, and I know many old soldiers who found it increasingly discomforting, year by year.'

After the parade of 1919, it was estimated that, if the ghosts of the dead soldiers had marched past the Cenotaph instead of those alive and weeping for lost comrades, it would have taken three and a half days for the parade of the lost to pass through. The construction of one memorial was not going to act as a permanent sop or succour to a population still struggling to come to terms with a world that seemed both indelibly altered, yet utterly unchanged. The promise of a better future for the working man and his family and new roles for women had not instantly materialised.

The British Government was not, however, unfeeling. Many of its members were similarly affected by grief and struggled to find the right answer for the nation. In 1917, whilst the war still raged and pressures were growing on the Home Front, a genuine concern for the bereaved was made a political imperative. Ministers wanted something to reinforce the view amongst the population that the huge numbers of men being killed or wounded were not fighting and dying in vain.

Rudyard Kipling had lost his 18-year-old son Jack at the Battle of Loos in 1915, and in Kipling, the government saw a public figure able to reinforce their message. A well-known and popular poet, he was also one of the bereaved, having lost a son to a war he had fervently believed in from the start. Kipling would, the government believed, offer sincerity and gravitas to a formulaic letter that was to be sent out to grieving relatives after the initial news of their loss had been transmitted by telegram.

As they quickly realised, those at the top levels of government had grossly underestimated the depth of Kipling's grief, his anger at the loss of his child and his reluctance to include those who had no similar experience. There could be no simple letter of condolence, Kipling stressed in his letter of reply. He wanted a medal, or badge, to be cast as a 'sign of distinction and (which is important) entails the wearer to look and talk with contempt at people who have not given their sons.' He wanted people who held on to what he referred to as 'lesser grievances' to feel discomfort at the sight of such a badge which, he felt, the bereaved 'would soon learn to wear' with pride. They would also, he envisaged, enjoy special church services and a place of honour when the necessary memorials to the war dead had been built.

The letter is astonishing in its exhibition of raw and undisguised contempt for anyone who did not share his experience. If Kipling had thought through the consequences of such a 'badge of honour' to its inevitable conclusion, then he would surely have realised how divisive such a medal would be, particularly in smaller communities. It would create discomfort and mark those for whom the end of the war was a cause for celebration, with brave and often decorated sons, brothers and fathers returned home, as somehow inadequate.

Not surprisingly, the idea was not acted upon by the government, although memorial plaques were sent to bereaved families. Kipling was not angry with the wider population whose sons had fought bravely and returned, perhaps gravely injured but alive, as his proposal seems to suggest, his anger was in fact with himself, for encouraging his son to join up. He felt he had as good as sacrificed him on the altar of his own pride and now he wanted a badge to somehow restore that pride and to offer a sense of community for those who had similar feelings. He was certainly not alone amongst a population that had waved young men goodbye in 1914 and encouraged them to believe in a war that later seemed futile. Many experienced similar guilt, along with those who had referred to young men returning shocked and damaged mentally as cowards and malingerers.

Those who had lost loved ones and those who had survived the war both experienced feelings of 'survivor guilt'. They had escaped death but would never properly come to terms with those feelings, or like Kipling, with the knowledge that they had pressed a son or husband to volunteer. It is a feeling better understood in the twenty-first century, but it still claims victims. On New Year's Day 2012, 29-year-old Lance Sergeant Daniel Collins, a soldier of the 1st Battalion the Welsh Guards, who had survived a tour of duty in Afghanistan despite being hit by a sniper's bullet, committed suicide. His own life had been saved by his body armour, but on the same tour Collins had lost two of his closest friends and although he had counselling and plans for his future he was, as his girlfriend said 'a very sensitive man who couldn't get past the guilt' of being the one who survived.

It is a guilt that can overwhelm not only individuals but whole families, communities and to a certain extent, a nation. Could this be why we still feel so drawn to mark the loss of the First World War in a way that is more melancholy and less proud than our commemorations of the Second?

Chapter Eight

The Legacy of Shell Shock: 1914–2014

Throughout history those in authority have tried to ensure that we do not see the harmful psychological effects of war as the normal response of either soldiers or civilians. They are right to say that war does not affect everyone in the same way. The vast majority of those in the twenty-first century armed forces are highly trained and able men and women, who are offered opportunities that civilian life could not give them. This book has not set out to establish that war trauma has left an indelible legacy on *all* families, or on *all* aspects of modern society. It has sought to highlight, however, the stresses endured by our recent ancestors and to encourage us to examine how our views of their quiet acceptance, silence or reluctance to share may be misplaced.

Post-1918 memoirs, poetry, novels and plays have examined the wider implications of the disillusionment that many felt between the wars. They suggest a brutal and unfeeling military and a Home Front and population that could not comprehend the horrors men went through. Many authors wanted to express their own horror at the way in which the First World War was conducted. Some were part of a circle of intellectuals who lost many friends in the war and were utterly unforgiving towards the authorities afterwards. There was a public outcry when the official number of those shot for cowardice or desertion was released. On hearing that 306 young men had been executed, there grew a sense of disquiet and a suspicion that brave young men were driven to desperate measures by old generals and politicians conducting the war from the safety of billets well behind the lines. Those writing of the war often expressed the feelings of the bereaved in a way they could not articulate themselves.

As the 1920s ended and the 1930s saw the rise of Fascism and the inexorable move towards another war, the horrors of the Great War were not forgotten and its consequences still affected many, but new fears distracted a new generation. The society that went to war in 1939 was very different to that of 1914, which had not yet shaken off Victorian and Edwardian sensibilities when it was called to arms.

For the armed forces, as war once more became likely, the need to ensure that future doctors did not face similar casualty rates from neurasthenia and shell shock was increasingly urgent. Doctors were keen to see how the diagnosing of mental illness' had developed and how it was now treated. In the 1930s greater weight was being given to the opinions of psychiatrists and psychologists. Doctors treating patients with war trauma had moved away from the disciplinary approach associated with cold baths and endless emotional pressure to conform, and towards one based more on the use of drugs (such as high dose barbiturates like sodium amytal or dangerously high levels of insulin) and electro-convulsive therapy, which was at this stage still crude. The most disturbing of the treatments, to modern eyes, is the surgical leucotomy, first undertaken in 1935. This neurosurgery, removing as it does some of the frontal lobes of the brain, has serious side-effects and has always been controversial, but it was used by many surgeons well into the 1970s to deal with mental health issues now treated simply by drugs.

World War Two and the Vietnam War created their own versions of shell shock. It might have been called combat fatigue or war neurosis but it had a similar effect on the victims. American veterans of the conflict in Vietnam seemed to find adapting to the society they returned to on demobilisation more difficult than those serving in previous wars. The symptoms experienced, similar to those of shell shock, metamorphosed into post-traumatic stress disorder (PTSD), which was at last recognised by the medical community in the 1980s. Historians began to reassess the experiences of soldiers in the trenches in the light of modern experience and writers such as Pat Barker rekindled interest in the phenomenon of shell shock in fiction.

Barker did a remarkable job of highlighting the way men had to repress a side of their personality to become brutal killers on the Front line; a dichotomy that came back to 'haunt' them in nightmares each night. The poet Wilfred Owen has been held up as the epitome of the sensitive young man who found himself forced to kill and to witness the suffering of his fellow men. How could this experience not have a lasting effect on a soldier's mental health? What proportion of those who went to war were unable to process these memories and later suffered enduring mental health problems? It is impossible to know now, but there are lessons to be learnt by the modern military. Even the most enthusiastic and committed recruit, man or woman, can succumb.

Of course we cannot judge those living 100 years ago by the standards of our own times. Even those of us lucky enough to have discussed the war with relatives, or as oral historians with survivors and their relatives, cannot get a truly accurate understanding of what life on both Fronts was like. But we are still human. We love, we grieve, we have our own anxieties, which have their own lasting effects on the psyche. We have much in common with our recent ancestors.

Over the twentieth century the meaning of shell shock evolved to suit the prevailing views of the time; but essentially it is seen as representative of injustice in wartime and as a symbol of lifelong war damage. Shell shock is always at the heart of remembrance of the Great War, despite those memoirs from veterans who came home apparently psychologically unscathed, having seen it all as a big adventure. Were they indeed simply repressing the horror, and in this case did it matter, if that is how they coped?

Men and women join the Forces for many different reasons and the challenges of modern military life, including institutionalisation, alcoholism, bullying and separation from family can be harder to cope with, especially if they are exposed to stressful combat situations. If they are injured, the inability to pursue their career and the psychological strain of dealing with disability can cause them to slip into a depression, especially if they face discharge and a return to civilian life, a transition many veterans find hard to adjust to.

Even now, service personnel are reluctant to seek help for mental health problems. They feel guilt and shame that they may be letting comrades down, or feel pressure to remain silent in what is still a very macho environment. Only three per cent of cases referred to the charity Combat Stress are made through the National Health Service; but overall, referrals have increased 66 per cent over the last six years. Those approaching the charity for help are, on average, men in their early to mid-forties who have served for around 10 years. Eighty two per cent are in the army, with only seven per cent in the navy.

For ex-soldiers after the Great War, their experience would be similar to that facing some twenty-first century veterans – family breakdown, unemployment, isolation and homelessness. After the Great War a common picture of the war veteran was as a man on the margins of society, a wanderer left rootless. For veterans of the modern armed forces, society's continued lack of understanding of their mental health needs is frustrating and dangerous. In the United States, where research into the needs of veterans is more advanced than in Britain, data suggests that 14 per cent of veterans experience PTSD or depression to such an extent that it impairs their functioning on a daily basis. One in eight has been addicted to alcohol and most disturbingly, a veteran commits suicide every 65 minutes in the US. An army veteran is twice as likely to commit suicide as a civilian.

Viktor E. Frankl, an Austrian psychiatrist who survived a Nazi concentration camp, wrote in *Man's Search for Meaning*: 'An abnormal reaction to an abnormal situation is normal behaviour.' This aphorism seems to suggest that a person who remains totally unaffected by their war experience should be described as 'abnormal'. To go through the horrors of the trenches, or challenges of life on the Home Front (or survive a Nazi concentration camp) without being indelibly altered, traumatised by sights and sounds of death or haunted by loss is the greater insanity.

As a leaflet published by the charity Combat Stress, the twenty-first century incarnation of the post Great War Ex-Servicemen's Welfare Society, states: 'The man who lost his life in Iraq, now lives in Birmingham.'

Bibliography

Appignanesi, Lisa, *Mad, Bad and Sad – A History of Women and the Mind Doctors from 1800 to the Present*, (Virago, 2009)

Arthur, Max, *Forgotten Voices of the Great War*, (Ebury, 2003)

Babington, Anthony, *Shell-Shock,* (Leo Cooper Ltd, 1997)

Barham, Peter, *Forgotten Lunatics of the Great War,* (Yale University Press, 2007)

Barker, Pat, *The Regeneration Trilogy*, (Viking, 2007)

Barrett, Michele, *Casualty Figures: How Five Men Survived the First World War*, (Verso, 2008)

Beckett, Ian, *Home Front 1914–1918 – How Britain Survived the Great War*, (The National Archives, 2006)

Beddoe, Deirdre, *Back to Home & Duty*, (Pandora Press 1989)

Bogacz, Ted, 'War Neurosis and Cultural Change in England 1914–1922: The Work of the War Office Committee of Enquiry into Shell Shock', *Journal of Contemporary History*, Vol. 24, No. 2, Studies on War, (Apr, 1989), pp. 227–256

Bourke, Joanna, *Dismembering the Male*, (University of Chicago Press, 1996)

Bourke, Joanna, 'Effeminacy, Ethnicity and the End of Trauma: The Sufferings of 'Shell Shocked' Men in Great Britain and Ireland 1914–1939', *Journal of Contemporary History*, Vol. 35, No. 1, Special Issue: Shell-Shock, (Jan. 2000), pp. 57–69

Brittain, Vera, *A Testament of Youth*, (Virago, 2004)

Brittain, Vera ed. Bostock, Mark, *Because You Died: Vera Brittain Poetry and Prose of the First World War and Beyond*, (Virago Press, 2010)

Fegan, Thomas, *The Baby Killers: German Raids on Britain in the First World War*, (Pen and Sword, 2002)

Graves, Robert, *Goodbye to All That*, (Penguin Classics, 2000)

Grayzel, Susan R., *Women and the First World War*, (Pearson, 2002)

Gregory, Adrian, *The Last Great War*, (Cambridge University Press, 2009)

Hall, Ruth, (ed) *Dear Dr Stopes: Sex in the 1920's*, (Andre Deutsch Limited, 1971)

Hanson, Neil, *First Blitz*, (Doubleday, 2008)

Hazelgrove, Jenny, *Spiritualism and British Society Between the Wars*, (Manchester University Press, 2000)

Heinl, Peter, *Splintered Innocence*, (Brunner Routledge, 2001)

Holden, Wendy, *Shell Shock, Traumatic Neurosis and the British Soldiers of the First World War*, (Channel Four Books, 1998)

Humphries, Steve and Van Emden, Richard, *All Quiet on the Home Front*, (Headline, 2004)

Hyde, Andrew, *The First Blitz 1917–1918*, (Pen and Sword, 2001)

Jones, Edgar and Wesseley, Simon, *Shell Shock to PTSD: Military Psychiatry from 1900 to the Gulf War*, (Psychology Press, 2005)

Jones, Edgar, 'War Neurosis and Arthur Hurst: A Pioneering Medical Film About the Treatment of Psychiatric Battle Casualties', *Journal of the History of Medicine and Allied Sciences* (May 2011), 67(3):345–73.

Jones, Edgar, 'Shell Shock at Maghull and the Maudsley: Models of Psychological Medicine in the UK', *Journal of the History of Medicine and Allied Sciences* (July 2010) 65 (3); 368–395

Jones, Edgar, Thomas, Adam, Ironside, Stephen, 'Shell shock: an outcome study of a First World War 'PIE' unit', *Psychological Medicine*, (2007), 37, 215–223.

Kingsley Kent, Susan, *Aftershocks: Politics and Trauma in Britain 1918–1931*, (Palgrave Macmillan, 2008)

Leed, Eric J., *No Man's Land: Combat and Identity in World War One*, (Cambridge University Press)

Leese, Peter, *Shell Shock, Traumatic Neurosis and the British Soldiers of the First World War*, (Palgrave Macmillan, 2002)

Leese, Peter, 'Problems Returning Home: The British Psychological Casualties of the Great War', *The Historical Journal*, 40, 4 (1997), pp 1055–67

McCaulay, Rose, *Non-Combatants and Others*, (Hodder and Stoughton, 1916)

Marwick, Arthur, *The Deluge: British Society in the First World War*, (Palgrave Macmillan, 2006)

Meyer, Jessica, *Men of War: Masculinity and the First World War in Britain*, (Palgrave Macmillan, 2009)

Nicholson, Julia, *The Great Silence: 1918–1920 Living in the Shadow of the Great War*, (John Murray, 2010)

Nicholson, Virginia, *Singled Out: How Two Million Women Survived Without Men After the First World War*, (Viking, 2007)

Oliver, Neil, *Not Forgotten*, (Hodder & Stoughton, 2005)

Overy, Richard, *The Morbid Age: Britain Between the Wars*, (Allen Lane, 2009)

Owen, Wilfred, *Collected Poems*, (Wordsworth Poetry Library, 1994)

PTSD Compensation and Military Service: Progress and Promise. Washington, D.C: National Academies Press. p. 35

Pugh, Martin, *We Danced All Night*, (Vintage, 2009)

Reid, Fiona, *Broken Men, Shell Shock, Treatment and Recovery in Britain 1914–1930*, (Continuum, 2011)

Roper, Michael, *The Secret Battle: Emotional Survival in the Great War*, (Manchester University Press, 2009)

Sassoon, Siegfried, *The Complete Memoirs of George Sherston*, (Faber & Faber, 1980)

Shepherd, Ben, *A War of Nerves: Soldiers and Psychiatrists 1914–1994*, (Pimlico, 2002)

Showalter, Elaine, *The Female Malady: Women, Madness and English Culture, 1830–1980*, (Virago, 1987)

Smith, Sir G.E and Pear, T.H., *Shell Shock and its Lessons*, (University Press, 1918)

Stallworthy, Jon, *Wilfred Owen*, (Oxford University Press, 1974)

Stevenson, John, *British Society 1914–1945*, (Penguin, 1990)

Todman, Dan, *The Great War: Myth and Memory*, (Hambledon Continuum, 2008)

Van Emden, Richard, *The Quick and the Dead*, (Bloomsbury, 2002)

Various, *The Penguin Book of First World War Poetry*, (Penguin Classics, 2006)

West, Rebecca, *The Return of the Soldier*, (Penguin, 1998)

Winter, Jay, 'Shell Shock and the cultural history of the Great War', *Journal of Contemporary History* (Jan 2000), vol. 35 no. 1 7–11

—— *Sites of Memory, States of Mourning*, (CUP 1998)

Woolf, Virginia, *Mrs Dalloway*, (Wordsworth Classics, 1996)

Archival Sources and Websites

.

The British Newspaper Archive
Digitised images from local and national newspapers from the 18th to 20th centuries.
Website: *www.britishnewspaperarchive.co.uk*

Great War Photos, WW1 Photos Centenary Website: 2014–2018
A wonderful photographic record and resource for the study of the First World War, collected by Paul Reed.
Website: *www.greatwarphotos.com*

The Imperial War Museum
IWM's online collections cover all aspects of twentieth and twenty-first century conflict involving Britain, the Commonwealth and other former empire countries.
Address: IWM London, Lambeth Road, London SE1 6HZ
IWM North, The Quays, Trafford Wharf Road, Trafford Park, Manchester M17 1TZ
Website: *www.iwm.org.uk/collections-research*

Islington Local History Centre
For detailed information about the population, housing and social history of the London Borough of Islington.
Address: Finsbury Library, 245 St John Street, London EC1V 4NB
Tel: 020 7527 7988
Website: *www.islington.gov.uk/islington/history-heritage/heritage*

Oxford University and JISC WW1 Centenary Open Educational Resource
Free online resources for teaching new perspectives on World War I
Website: *http://ww1centenary.oucs.ox.ac.uk*

Picture the Past
'Picture the Past' conserves, and makes accessible online, the photographic heritage of the North East Midlands, including photos of the impact of the Great War on the local area.
Website: *www.picturethepast.org.uk*

University of Leeds, Special Collections – Liddle Collection
The Liddle Collection includes the personal papers of more than 4,000 people who lived through the First World War.
Address: The Brotherton Library, University of Leeds, Leeds LS2 9JT
Tel: 0113 343 5518
Website: *http://library.leeds.ac.uk/liddle-collection*

The Wellcome Library
Contains a wide range of books and articles on the subject of shell shock and the development of psychiatric medicine.
Address: 183 Euston Road, London NW1 2BE
Website: *http://wellcomelibrary.org*

Index